WASHINGTON - ROCHAMBEAU

REVOLUTIONARY ROUTE

and the

Franco-American Alliance

DONNA PASSMORE   JAN SMULCER

For information contact Values Through History, Sugar Land, TX 77478

ISBN 978-0-692-96044-8

This publication was made possible by

the financial support and encouragement of the

American Society of the French Legion of Honor

in partnership with

The Society of the Cincinnati

and

Values Through History

Our special thanks go to

Jay W. Jackson

Honorable Guy N. Wildenstein

Ambassador Jean-David Levitte

Raynald, Duc de Choiseul Praslin

Hamelin, Comte de La Grandière

Ellen Clark

Henry Fishburne

Preston Russell

Introduction

Thousands of professional French soldiers, led by General Rochambeau and commanded by General Washington, fought on American soil for this nation's independence. Thousands of sailors in the French navy fought at sea, and France gave staggering sums in support for years. Without these great contributions and the will of France, American victory may well not have been the outcome of the American Revolution. In commemoration, the Washington-Rochambeau National Historical Trail has been created. It follows the land routes that the allied armies traversed at great speed despite formidable conditions, and stretches from Rhode Island to victory in Yorktown.

The actual events of the Franco-American Alliance are more improbable and dramatic than fiction, and the narrative that follows tells that story. At the end of each chapter, the locations mentioned within that chapter are listed and numbered to assist your finding them on the included foldout map. This map is a somewhat simplified version of a map brilliantly drawn by General Rochambeau's staff to meet the needs of a marching army.

After the narrative, in the Appendix, the manual presents sites and other aids for anyone wishing to retrace some or all of the Washington-Rochambeau Revolutionary Route. Please consider the offerings as highlights; there are already more than we list, and communities along the over six-hundred-mile route continue to add resources of interest to historical travellers. The webpages listed in the section will also help you expand what each area along the trail can offer you as you travel.

Jean-Baptiste Donatien de Vimeur,

comte de Rochambeau

Contents

The Story

of the

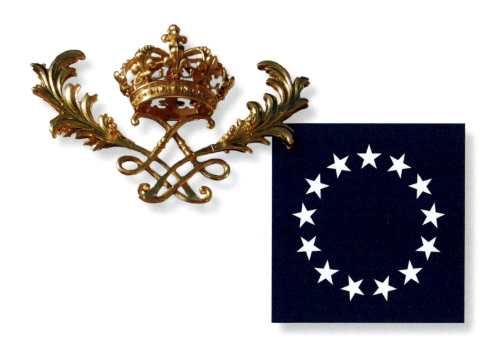

Franco-American

ALLIANCE

DEANE · ROYAL MOTIVES · HORTALEZ & CIE

American Response to de Bonvouloir's Message

The impact of Bonvouloir's mission was significant on both sides of the Atlantic. In America, Congress's secret committee prepared to send Connecticut Congressman Silas Deane to the Court of France as a covert representative of the Continental Congress. Simultaneously they reached out to Arthur Lee, the colonial agent for Pennsylvania in London, to learn the attitudes of European rulers toward the Patriots.

French Leaders' Motives in Helping America

In France, Bonvouloir's report added weight to Vergennes's proposed strategy. King Louis XVI of France and his cabinet were not enchanted by the ideas of natural rights and self-rule that inspired the American Patriots, and they found it appalling that people would revolt against their king. Greater than their repugnance, however, was their hunger to see Britain humbled. Since losing the French and Indan War in 1763, France had craved revenge. Foreign Minister Choiseul and his successor Vergennes saw Americans as a means to achieve that retribution. These ministers had been secretly monitoring the rising conflict, hoping that war between America and Britain would break out and last for years. If England were to fight a long, expensive war against an enemy an ocean away, it would be impoverished and its military weakened. Even better, if after all those years England were to lose, whoever had helped the Americans win could reasonably expect to grow rich from all the American trade previously controlled by England. Determined to become that "friend to America," the king authorized the creation of a private business behind whose front France would act.

Étienne-François, comte de Stainville, duc de Choiseul

Roderique Hortalez et Cie

The shell company Roderigue Hortalez et Cie had been the brainchild of Pierre-Augustin Caron de Beumarchais, an Enlightenment dramatist, American fan, and elite French agent often in London. Beumarchais was named to run it, and then Louis XVI and his cousin Charles III of Spain each contributed one million *livres*. In his instructions to Beaumarchais, Vergennes said:

The operation must have essentially in the eyes of the British Government, and even in the eyes of the Americans, the aspect of an individual speculation, to which we are strangers.... With these two millions, you shall found a great commercial establishment, and at your own risk and peril you shall furnish to America arms and everything else necessary to sustain war. Our arsenals will deliver to you arms and munitions, but you shall pay for them. You will not demand money of the Americans for they have none; but you can ask return in their staple products.

On July 4, 1776, Hortalez et Cie opened for business in Paris. Beaumarchais enlisted the "private American citizen" Silas Deane to help as they obtained and hid the first shipments of materiel (military supplies and equipment) that America needed. They then searched out ships and captains willing to take on the dangers of transporting these goods to officially neutral Caribbean islands or directly to Patriot-held North American ports.

Because British observers and ships were actively searching for French involvement, it took months for the goods to make it out of port and even longer to arrive in America. Some shipments were lost enroute. The first shipment did not arrive in Portsmouth, New Hampshire until March 1777.

Beaumarchais

Naval Support of American Ships in France, the Rest of Europe, and on the Open Seas

Even after Britain declared the Americans to be in rebellion, France continued and escalated a longstanding tradition of working with American ships, despite the dangers. French ports usually remained open to Americans, French and Spanish ships sometimes shielded American vessels from the British on the high seas, and complaints from irate British officials were generally met with plausible explanations or ignored.

Popular Support of America in France

The people of France shared their king's thirst for revenge, but they also backed America because it epitomized enlightened self-governance that protected individuals' natural and inalienable rights. The very idea that distant English colonies were actually fighting to become a republic based on these ideals generated great fervor.

One consequence was a steady stream of military men who wanted to fight for America appearing on Silas Deane's doorstep. They asked for letters of introduction, promises of pay and rank, and sometimes even money for passage, and Deane gave most of them what they requested. Vergennes, desperate to remain below the radar of Britain, discouraged public expressions of support for America but could not completely contain them.

Need for Support Increases and Benjamin Franklin Goes to France

By the end of summer in 1776, America had declared its independence, but Washington's army had been chased from New York City and their prospects looked dim. Though the promise of military supplies was comforting to those who knew about Hortalez et Cie, nothing had arrived yet, and America needed help desperately. Unfortunately, Deane had been unable to obtain greater commitments. In October 1776, a month after adopting the name "United States" for the country, Congress sent seventy-year-old Benjamin Franklin to France to try to convince that nation to do more. Franklin, Deane, and Arthur Lee became the American Commission in France. That same month, Hortalez et Cie shipped clothing and muskets for 20,000 men, gunpowder, cannons, shot and shells.

Louis XVI Privately Receives the American Commission

Benjamin Franklin was one of the most famous men in the world, revered throughout Europe, except in England. He personified science and the Enlightenment. With Franklin's arrival, French popular support for America soared. His brilliance, wit and charisma were irresistible. In December 1776, a few days after Franklin arrived in Paris, the American Commission was invited to privately meet with Louis XVI for the first time. This meeting was significant because symbolically it was one country talking to another country, not dialogue between individuals. Finally, the American Commission was able to speak

as the United States of America to assure Vergennes and the King that the nation desired a formal alliance with France. They also talked plainly about the types of help the Patriots needed. Among these were skilled military engineers, money, weapons, ammunition, uniforms, and especially the force of the French navy. Almost immediately, four outstanding French military engineers departed for America via the Caribbean under assumed names.

News of the brilliant victories at Trenton and Princeton caused rejoicing throughout France, and in the spring of 1777, the King and his ministers were almost ready to sign a treaty. Yet they hesitated, still waiting for Spain to join them openly before committing to an act that would incite England to declare war. In the meantime, French aid poured out in the form of goods (partially purchased with Spanish funds), officers, and protection of American ships in Caribbean waters.

Lafayette.

LAFAYETTE · HESITATION · SARATOGA · TREATIES

Lafayette

Among the French officers who passionately wanted to fight for America was an extraordinary young noble, Marie-Joseph Paul Yves Roch Gilbert du Motier, Marquis de Lafayette. Lafayette believed fervently in the values for which America was fighting, and so admired Washington that he bought and refitted a fine ship, hired a crew, and sailed to America. At first Congress rejected him because many of the foreign volunteers sent by Deane had caused nothing but problems. Lafayette's sincerity, along with his willingness to lead no troops and receive no pay if only he could serve in Washington's command, changed their minds. In August, he met Washington for the first time. Washington had been reluctant to bring a teenaged, foreign noble into his military staff, but instantly upon meeting, the American commander and the nineteen-year-old bonded like father and son. That meeting began a lifelong relationship of critical importance not just to the two men but also to the future of two nations.

French Hesitation

As 1777 progressed, news from America darkened. The American Commissioners in Paris were able to highlight the good news and downplay the bad until Philadelphia fell in September. With that loss, French leaders worried that they were making a serious mistake in siding with the Patriots.

Saratoga

Finally, in early December 1777, encouraging news arrived. Thousands of British troops had surrendered unconditionally at Saratoga, New York. While the French press remained silent to "prove" the nation's neutrality, spontaneous celebrations spread with the speed of the fastest messengers. The fact that the victorious Americans had been clothed and armed from the first shipments sent by Hortalez & Cie was particularly gratifying to those in France who knew. In fact, during 1777, five million *livres* worth of supplies had been sent to America. Immediately the Commission again asked for a treaty with France, spicing their request with news that London was suddenly making settlement offers to Congress. If France intended to make a greater commitment, they needed to say so right away.

The Treaties

On December 17, 1777, the Commission learned that Louis XVI of France would formally enter into an alliance. France would ask for absolutely "nothing which the Americans would regret in the future," even though the alliance would immediately bring a world war upon France.

Franco-American
ALLIANCE

King Louis XVI of France

On February 6, 1778, France and the United States signed two treaties, one public, one private. In the public one, the Treaty of Amity and Commerce, France recognized the United States as a free and independent nation and established trade between the countries. In the secret pact, the Treaty of Alliance, France agreed to fight the British for American independence if Britain declared war on France. In return, the United States promised to continue the war until its independence was recognized by England and committed to ensure that France would keep its Caribbean islands. Both countries promised that neither ally would sign a peace treaty unless the other agreed.

Most of the leaders across Europe believed that France had made a horrific, stupid mistake.

The people of France, however, celebrated joyously.

TREATY OF ALLIANCE

Immediate Consequences of the Treaty

King George III of England

On March 13, 1778, just over a month after the Franco-American treaties were signed, the British learned what had transpired. King George III, members of Parliament, and the ministers raged. Both countries recalled their ambassadors, a signal of war. For a time, though, the British did not attack.

One week after London was informed of the treaties, Louis XVI publicly recognized the United States and by this act proclaimed France the ally of America.

Americans learned the incredible news early in May 1778. The French were with them! A fleet was coming! Celebrations and thankful religious services went on for days, yet there were worries as well. How would these two military cultures work together? When would they come? Could France really be trusted not to try to seize power? Hopes outweighed fears, but everyone believed the union would present challenges. For the time being, though, the promise of coming help sustained the Patriots and figured into their strategies.

The British military in America was deeply alarmed when they were informed of the treaties. The British immediately abandoned Philadelphia, under orders to return to New York City. Washington's men dogged their column and engaged in one major battle, trying to buy time for the French fleet to arrive and prevent the British navy from supporting British troops.

The plan was for Washington's soldiers to threaten New York City in order to keep the British navy from racing to Newport during a specific period. The French navy and other American units were to use that time to defeat and take the British base in Newport. American Brigadier General John Sullivan was to command a land attack tightly coordinated with d'Estaing's naval artillery attack. Washington had reservations about the hot-tempered and prejudiced Sullivan who loathed all French people, but he could not replace him. He co-assigned Lafayette, the only Frenchman whom Sullivan liked, and Nathanael Greene, an outstanding general, hoping they could keep Sullivan's personality in check. The action was set to begin at the end of July 1778.

The operation failed, though not by any fault of d'Estaing. Washington's men kept the British army and navy tied down in New York for all of the agreed days, and d'Estaing was ready in ample time, but Sullivan ran late. By the time the operation began, the British fleet was en route from New York. The French fleet had made it past British cannons into the confines of the bay when Howe's larger British force appeared over the horizon, changing everything. D'Estaing had to meet them in open sea to have even a chance of surviving, let alone winning. Out they went, under fire from British batteries, but the British ships, warned by the cannons, fled, and the French followed. A fierce gale badly damaged the fleet, and though they limped back to Newport ten days later, d'Estaing refused to reengage until his vessels were repaired in Boston. Sullivan was furious. His hateful words and letters heaped all the blame on the French. Loyalists spread these letters, inciting riots in Boston and even the death of one French military man.

This appalling treatment of the French was a national disgrace that could have easily driven away the one country whose help was essential. Lafayette raced to Boston to tell the truth of the matter and to ask the leaders there to do all they could to sway public opinion before permanent damage was done. Washington immediately sent his sincere apologies to d'Estaing and others, and strongly urged Sullivan to repair the harm he had caused. Respected Patriots in Boston, John Hancock foremost among them, went to great lengths to treat the French navy well and led others in the same direction. The Hancocks and their friends wined and dined d'Estaing and his many officers constantly while the ships were being repaired, culminating in a splendid reception at Faneuil Hall with about 500 prominent Bostonians present. As thirteen gun salutes boomed, they roared their toasts to the United States and the King of France.

For his part, d'Estaing rose above the insults, defending his actions while even offering to serve in the army as a colonel under General Sullivan. That did not happen, but Sullivan backed off and the alliance held. Newport, however, was controlled more tightly than ever by the British, and d'Estaing had to sail for the Caribbean as soon as the repairs were made. The Americans were once more without the help of the French fleet, without any significant gains achieved.

Charles Hector, comte d'Estaing

SAVANNAH ·
LAFAYETTE · FRENCH CAMPAIGN

A Difficult Year

The year 1778 that had started with such hope drew to its end bleakly for the Patriots. Without enough funds, supplies, or soldiers, there had been little Washington could do. Battles that had taken place were either losses or victories of little strategic importance. Indians massacred settlements in upper New York, and American privateer ships and stores were destroyed in New Jersey.

The British Take Savannah

During this same period, the British were also discouraged because they, too, had made no real progress. Unlike the Patriots, though, they had the means to try something new. In late December 1778, the British captured Savannah, Georgia, restarting a southern campaign. Washington's army was impossibly far away, locked down in winter camps near New York City, menacing but rarely engaging the British.

1779 Lafayette Champions America in France

The next year, 1779, was even grimmer. Early in the year, Lafayette returned home. There he worked tirelessly, pressing for increased support for the war, but few in America were aware of his efforts. What they did know was that American money was nearly worthless, Congress was ineffective, and Washington was struggling to keep his army functioning. Small victories and defeats in the North continued without meaningful results. In the South the British were winning, sweeping westward in Georgia and northward into South Carolina.

Spain, John Paul Jones, and Ambassador Luzerne

Some good news finally came from Europe, and American leaders spread it to keep national morale from plummeting. On June 21, 1779, Spain had entered the war, stretching the British navy even thinner. Captain John Paul Jones was successfully attacking British ships and driving their navy to distraction along

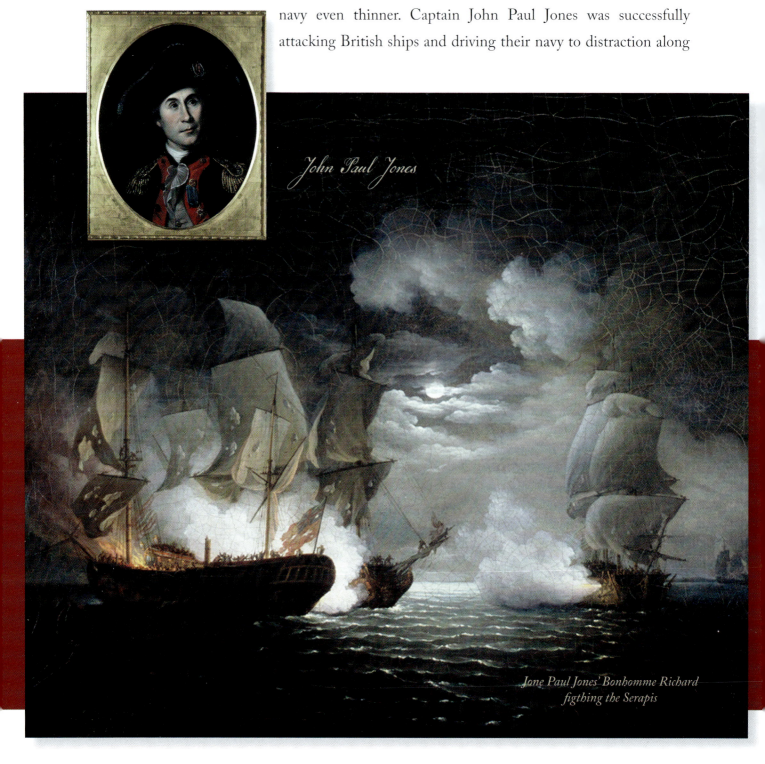

John Paul Jones

Jone Paul Jones' Bonhomme Richard figthing the Serapis

the British coast. Late in the year a new Minister to the United States, Anne-César de La Luzerne, arrived from France. Americans hoped he would prove to be the effective advocate and friend the Patriots needed.

Admiral d'Estaing and the Siege of Savannah

In response to the Patriots' desperate call for help in Savannah, in early September 1779, d'Estaing sailed in from the Caribbean carrying outstanding French regiments from the islands. He arrived well before the Patriot land forces were ready, however, and could not wait. Though the French and Americans battled valiantly to free the city, the operation was badly coordinated and ended in terrible losses and defeat. Despite the outcome, d'Estaing and his men earned and, unlike what happened in Newport, received gratitude and respect for their valor. Unfortunately, though, the only positive news Versailles received from America for months was the Patriots' appreciation for d'Estaing and the admiration of the new ambassador for Washington.

In late December 1779, General Henry Clinton, British Commander-in-Chief in North

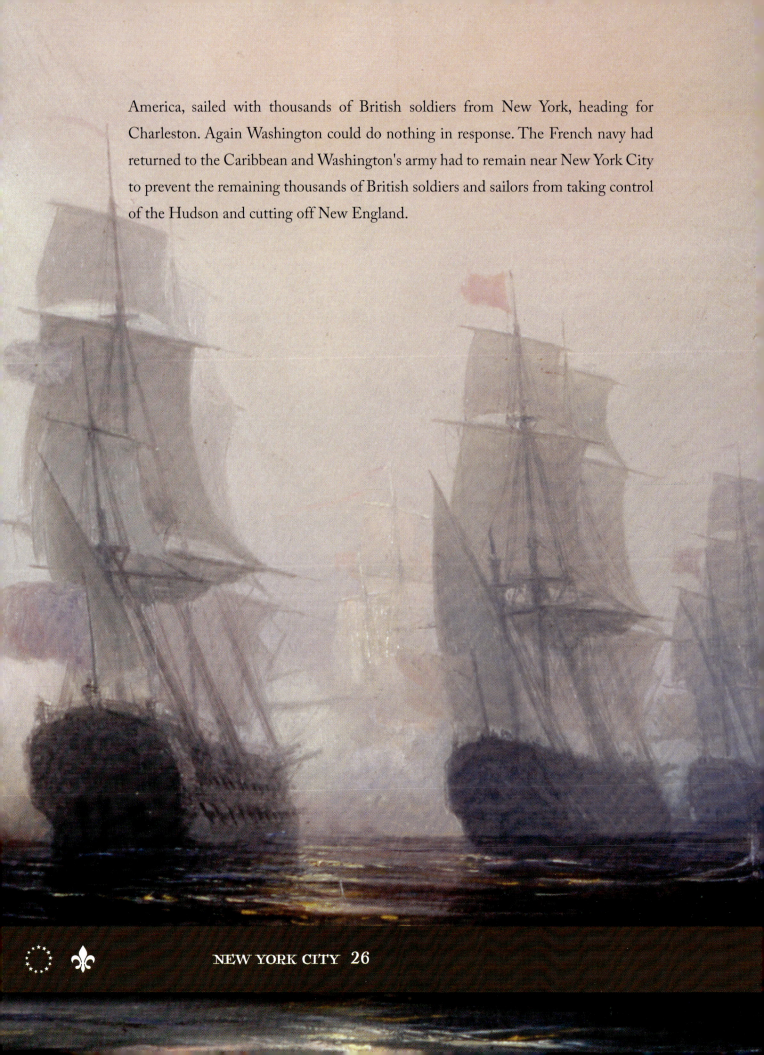

America, sailed with thousands of British soldiers from New York, heading for Charleston. Again Washington could do nothing in response. The French navy had returned to the Caribbean and Washington's army had to remain near New York City to prevent the remaining thousands of British soldiers and sailors from taking control of the Hudson and cutting off New England.

MILITARY COMMITMENT ·
ROCHAMBEAU

Mutual Disappointment

During the winter of 1779-1780, the Continental Army suffered the harshest physical conditions of the entire war. Through the freezing months the soldiers received a small fraction of the rations they needed, and morale plummeted.

As Americans viewed it, the past two years of the alliance with France had not even come close to expectations. As France viewed it, America depended far too much on France. Both countries realized that the ability of the Patriots to sustain their cause looked less likely in the spring of 1780 than it had in 1778.

L'Expédition Particulière

Thanks in large part to Lafayette's unrelenting efforts and French public support, things were about to change for the better. Lafayette convinced the ministers and King that Patriots would welcome French soldiers in addition to naval help, and France committed to provide the needed forces as well as materiel and money. In February 1780, the decision was made that France would send an army of relief to be placed wholly at Washington's disposal, a vast fleet, and an outright gift of six million *livres* as soon as possible. The codename for this great mobilization was the *Expédition Particulière*.

Lafayette was granted the honor of carrying the news. He left immediately on the swift ship *l'Hermione*, evaded the British navy, and arrived at Washington's Morristown, New Jersey headquarters on May 2, 1780, with his astounding message. He brought hope at the eleventh hour, and the news sent a shock of energy throughout the nation.

l'Hermione

Washington made the most of the announcement by pairing it with his own urgent call for state support. Americans realized the strategic importance of their army being strong, large, and well outfitted by the time of the French arrival. Supply levels, attitudes and recruitment finally began to improve, and the army almost doubled, reaching 15,000 men. In gratitude, Congress awarded Lafayette his own command of 2,000 American troops.

The news sustained Patriot spirits through the devastating fall of Charleston on May 12, 1780, the biggest American loss of the war.

Defeat at Charleston

Jean Baptiste Donatien de Vimeur,

comte de Rochambeau

General Rochambeau

Jean Baptiste Donatien de Vimeur, comte de Rochambeau was the commander chosen to lead the army of *Expédition Particulière.* The ministers and king had chosen exceptionally well. Rochambeau was a veteran of over forty years experience with a record of outstanding performance. Though born a noble, he was a soldier's soldier, an officer of honor whom his men trusted completely. His nickname among his troops was "Papa Rochambeau," and his men were always the best trained in the army. One experience in the European campaigns of the Seven Years War made him the ideal commander of the *Expédition Particulière.* In that conflict, he had witnessed horrific results that followed when his commanders had put their egos first. They had not planned or communicated well together; men died needlessly, and a war was lost. Now he was to serve under an American general much less experienced than he, while retaining command of his own soldiers. He was absolutely determined to make that work.

Troops and Departure

Rochambeau was promised six outstanding regiments plus artillery, totaling 8,000 men, a force he considered to be the minimum needed for success. To a man, these soldiers were afire with the idea of coming to the aid of the land of liberty, battling the British, and earning glory. They could hardly wait. Rochambeau completed his preparations efficiently, and for weeks the soldiers and masses upon masses of equipment waited at the port for enough ships to gather.

Already the naval war against Britain was being fought in the Mediterranean, along the coasts of Africa and Europe, in the Indian Ocean, and in the Caribbean, so the French navy was stretched thin. Assembling enough sound transport ships to carry the entire expedition, its supplies, and equipment proved impossible.

Because the troops had to carry virtually everything they would need in America, only 5,500 soldiers could be crammed aboard the available ships. Competition to be included was fierce among the men, even resulting in violence. As the 10 warships and 32 transports under the command of Admiral de Ternay were weighing anchor, some of the left-behind soldiers tried to board by climbing ropes. "Soon," they were told while being forced back. Both they and their generals were counting on the truth of that assurance.

The soldiers on board included more engineers, two companies of artillery, four highly decorated regiments, and the smaller Légion Volontaires Etrangers de Lauzun (Lauzun's Legion), all led by men from noble families. Lafayette's brother-in-law, vicomte de

Noialles, and Rochambeau's son, vicomte de Rochambeau, were both second-in-command of regiments. Most of the officers were men of considerable military experience and tradition.

No sooner had the ships sailed beyond their moorings than a strong contrary wind arose. It blew the wrong way for weeks, allowing them to go nowhere. Finally, on May 3, 1780, the day after Washington had learned they were coming, Rochambeau's army sailed out to the open sea. Almost immediately, a violent storm crashed upon them and scattered the fleet, but instead of creating a bad beginning, the storm served them well. They were unharmed, and that same storm saved them from the British because it kept Admiral Graves's faster ships in port for two weeks.

Daily Sea Rations for the Common Soldier or Sailor

½ lb. of bread or hardtack three times a day at 7 am, noon, 6 pm

0.6 pound of very salty salted beef or ham served once daily at noon

Soybean (or similar) soup (unspecified amount) flavored with oil once daily at supper

½ cup of red wine OR 2 tablespoons of liquor served 3 times daily with meal

½ cup water per day

French Regimental Colors

Royal Deux-Ponts

Saintonge

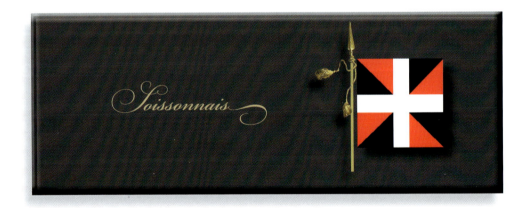

Soissonnais

Lauzun's Legion

Hypothetical standard (based on
Lauzun's coat of arms)

FRENCH ARMY ARRIVAL

Rochambeau's Army Arrives at Newport

On July 11, 1780, after seventy days at sea, the French sailed into Newport, Rhode Island. Silence, closed doors, and shuttered windows demonstrated the feelings of the residents.

Years of living under British wartime control had been very unpleasant. Not only that, but the number of armed men on the ships was as much as the whole population of Newport, so the prospect of even a friendly occupation of the town was daunting to the citizens.

They had been fed such negative information that many expected the Frenchmen would spit upon the American cause and ideals and would connive to seize America for France. They would demand, seduce, lie, and steal whatever they wanted—goods, homes, daughters, and wives. General Rochambeau had expected this negative attitude, but many of his officers were shocked and deeply offended. Clermont-Crèvecœur summed it up, "We inspired the greatest terror in them…. [T]he local people…would have preferred, at that moment, I think, to see their enemies arrive rather than their Allies."

Washington had assigned a thousand men to protect the arrival because he feared a negative response by civilians, but that first day Rochambeau began reversing preconceptions. He went ashore and personnally assured the townspeople that his forces would pay handsomely and promptly in silver and gold for all they required, and his men would behave with good manners and restraint. Naturally, word traveled quickly, and the townspeople's worries diminished dramatically.

The following morning, a high-ranking Continental officially welcomed the French, and that night the whole city welcomed them with a "grand illumination," candles glowing in all the visible windows facing the harbor, a rare extravagance in this war-worn city.

The very next day, once the men were all ashore, Rochambeau sent a message to Washington at his headquarters west of New York City:

My master's orders place me at the disposal of your excellency. I am arrived full of submission and zeal, and of veneration for yourself and for the talents you have shown in sustaining a war that will be forever memorable.

Washington's letter in reply was its match and included these words:

I hasten to communicate with you with what happiness I have received news of your safe arrival and in my name and in the name of the American Army I present to you the assurance of my deep appreciation and my lively gratitude to the Allies who have come so generously to our aid.

The men were in relatively good shape when they arrived, but that did not mean they were well. Over the course of the 70-day trip, nearly 200 men had died and their bodies quietly slipped out through the portholes at night. On arrival about 800 soldiers and 1,500 sailors were suffering from scurvy, and in some 100-man companies only 18-20 men were fit enough to work. The people of Newport "had very great pity on them and did all they could for them," and most recovered, but it took several weeks for most of the army to return to full fitness. During those weeks, the men and equipment were sorted, fortifications were built and strengthened, and good relationships were established with the locals.

Winning Hearts and Minds

The lower ranking soldiers were key in establishing those positive relationships. Their behavior was so superior to that of the British that the locals were astounded, and most tensions in the area simply disappeared.

Parents of young women, however, remained fearful. The elegant Frenchmen were enchanting, and some parents locked away their daughters to protect their hearts and virtue. To their credit, most Frenchmen showed unprecedented restraint.

INDIANS · ONE-ON-ONE · ARNOLD'S BETRAYAL

Preventing British-Indian Alliance

Tied down in Newport, Rhode Island by a British naval squadron, Rochambeau's troops spent the late summer and fall of 1780 strengthening themselves and their position. In late August, they also had an unexpected opportunity to persuade some northern Indians not to side with the British. A group of Indians arrived in Newport, representatives of several tribes who had long been allies of the French. The British, trying to entice Indians to fight against the Patriots, had assured them that the French were in no way helping the Americans. The Indians had come to learn the truth.

The French honored them with resplendent parades, artillery, a tour of a ship, and more. Rochambeau received them formally and General Heath held a feast in their honor. The Indians in turn demonstrated a war dance and bloodless scalping demonstrations. One Indian asked Rochambeau why "the children of their king" (the French army) were helping "the children of the enemy king" (the Patriots). Rochambeau replied that the enemy king (King George III) had treated these children so badly that they had cried out to the French king for help, and he felt compelled to come to their aid. That satisfied the Indians, and the visit was a complete success. Rochambeau for a time had ensured their neutrality.

Washington, Lafayette, and Rochambeau

From French arrival in July through early September 1780, the most important relationship, that between Washington and Rochambeau, was unintentionally being strained. Duties and lack of funds forced Washington to remain with his army in New York, almost a week's travel from Newport. As a result, he had assigned Lafayette to liaise with Rochambeau. Washington had no idea that his well-meaning go-between was driving Rochambeau and his veteran officers mad with overzealous proposals for impossible missions. Rochambeau did not complain about Lafayette, but eventually he told Washington that they needed to meet.

Meeting at Hartford

Washington agreed immediately. Their first meeting was on September 21, 1780, in Hartford, Connecticut, midpoint between camps. Success depended upon these commanders and their men working well together. Neither general expected a final plan to come from this meeting, but each needed to divulge matters of concern and find areas of agreement. Rochambeau explained that he was still far short of promised men, funds, and materiel, facts that embarrassed him. Washington admitted that the American army was desperately lacking in everything, and promoted his idea of an attack on the British in New York. Rochambeau spoke no English and Washington spoke no French, so Lafayette served as careful translator.

The commanders discovered that they sincerely liked and respected one another, and they worked well together. Washington listened carefully, as was his way, and Rochambeau was the epitome of diplomatic professionalism. Both received the other's admissions with grace. When Washington learned that the French opposed a major engagement until both armies had ample troops as well as naval superiority, he accepted their judgment though it delayed decisive action until spring. The French commander promised that his own son, vicomte de Rochambeau, would sail immediately and carry their joint request to Louis XVI for more men, a great fleet, and money to ensure they could indeed make that attack.

The French aides were also favorably impressed with their allied commander-in-chief. Count von Fersen, whose opinions were sometimes sharply critical, wrote of Washington:

His face is handsome and majestic but at the same time kind and gentle; corresponding completely with his moral qualities. He looks like a hero; he is very cold and says little but he is frank and polite. There is a sadness in his countenance which does not misbecome him and indeed renders his face more interesting.

Betrayal at West Point

While the generals were conferring, a messenger raced in with the news that many more British ships had arrived in New York harbor. Believing an attack on Newport might well be imminent, both parties immediately set out for their respective encampments. En route, Washington stopped at West Point, the critical fortress that held the Hudson River against the British. He discovered the post was barely defended and its commander, General Benedict Arnold, was missing. Washington had arrived in the midst of Arnold's treason, his attempt to deliver West Point and thus the Hudson River to the enemy in exchange for personal rank and riches. Though Washington and his men were devastated by the immensity of Arnold's betrayal, they flew into action to prevent the fortress from being taken, though Arnold escaped. Throughout the nation, the blow of Arnold's treachery produced a galvanizing force of outrage, hatred, and fury.

M.G Benedict Arnold

British Major John Andre is captured carrying the plans of West Point given to him by Arnold.

In the French Camp

Rochambeau's son sailed immediately for France, and the British naval attack on Newport did not happen. Many months passed relatively uneventfully as the men of France waited for the rest of their army to arrive.

SOUTHERN TIDES · SECOND THOUGHTS · LAURENS IN FRANCE

Kings Mountain Victory and Nathanael Greene Takes the Southern Command

In early October 1780, a major Patriot victory on Kings Mountain, South Carolina began to turn the tide in the South for the Patriots. Soon after, Washington sent General Nathanael Greene, whom he considered to be the best general in the whole army, to lead the Southern Army. As winter came, at least there was reason to hope.

General Nathanael Greene

Dark Winter of the Northern Armies

In the North, the stalemate held through the winter of 1780-1781. As the British army wintered in comfort in New York City once again, Washington could not even pay for courier service from his New Windsor, New York headquarters to Rochambeau. Emotional fatigue affected the country, and the spirit of the Continentals was dying. The French soldiers were also frustrated. They chafed as autumn became winter and still there was no call to arms. The boredom of camp life, the stress of being foreigners, and concern about the mettle of their American allies undermined their spirits. However, Washington's Continentals were experiencing far worse problems.

Mutinies broke out among American troops and had to be quashed. Washington begged repeatedly for payroll on behalf of his men, but Congress provided nothing. The general fought daily to preserve his army, using every scrap of good news and every other means available to support his men in body and morale. Both he and Rochambeau marked time through the long, bleak winter, desperately hoping that the needed French armada, men, and money would appear in the spring so at last they would have the capacity to achieve a decisive victory.

Cowpens and Arnold in Virginia

Fortunately, in January heartening news came from South Carolina. Part of Greene's army under Daniel Morgan had decisively beaten Bloody Tarleton, the most fearsome of Cornwallis's commanders, at the Battle of the Cowpens.

That same month, America learned that the

General Daniel Morgan

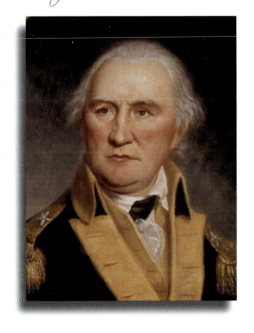

traitor Benedict Arnold was leading a British attack force through Virginia. In the first week, they seized Portsmouth and then destroyed the ironworks and warehouses of Richmond, burning much of the city. Arnold's intent, beyond terrorizing, was to prevent army goods from going south and to seize or destroy all income-producing products. Despite the best efforts of the small militias in Virginia, General Greene's men in the Carolinas were soon dangerously handicapped by lack of needed supplies.

Lafayette to Virginia

In February 1781, Washington sent Lafayette in command of approximately 1,200 men to Virginia to help stop Arnold.

Dire Straights in the North

As winter thawed into spring in 1781 and British ships prowled off Newport, Washington and Rochambeau prepared as best they could for what they hoped would be a decisive season. It had to be. As the mutinies demonstrated, the length of time without proper pay, food, clothing, equipment, or significant success was destroying the American army, and inactivity had begun to harm the French as well.

Vergennes Wants an End

Back in Versailles, the stark condition of the French treasury and the time and money already invested in the war with no victory in sight caused Foreign Mininster Vergennes to rethink his country's commitment. He privately considered negotiating a peace treaty that would not include American independence. Vergennes began arranging the peace summit, and talk of it made its way to America, though without even a whisper about sacrificing America's freedom. America, too, was so very weary of the war. Everyone hoped peace could be reached through diplomacy, but the Patriots did not believe that peace without independence was acceptable or think it would ever be considered.

John Laurens at Versailles

In the meantime, Washington sent his talented aide, multilingual John Laurens, as a special emissary to remind French leaders that without greater support, the American army would soon collapse.

In March 1781, Laurens arrived in France and with his passionate, direct approach insulted the Minister of the Navy practically with his first breath. He said that he was obligated to France,

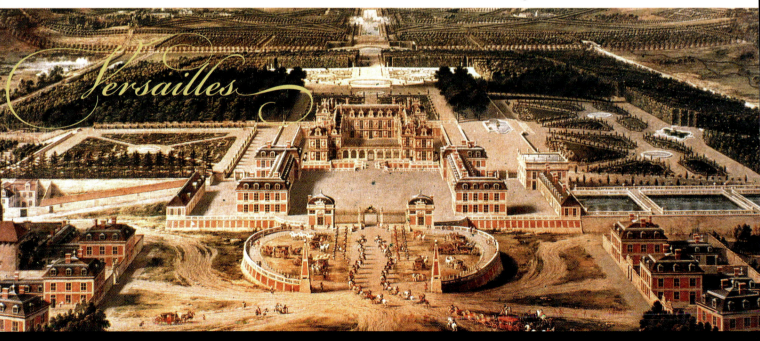

> …but, my sword which I now wear in defense of France as well as my own country, unless the [help] I solicit is immediately accorded, I may be compelled to draw against France as a British subject.

Vergennes was apoplectic. Benjamin Franklin was appalled and very fearful of what this threat could do to relations with France. Young Laurens, however, was not done. He passed a note directly to King Louis XVI at a social function, something that shattered the all-but-sacred rules of protocol. The shocked monarch stared at the note in his hand and then passed it to his Minister of War, and turned away. The very next day the finance minister informed Laurens that a huge shipment of supplies and some of the funding he had so forcefully demanded would be delivered immediately. Having accomplished his mission, Laurens apologized profusely for being "a soldier, little acquainted with the usages of court but warmly attached to my country."

The fear of the Americans uniting with Britain against France had been one reason the French had gone to war in the first place. Franklin had led in creating and maintaining the crucial relationships and interest. Lafayette had brought more pressure to bear. Finally, it was Laurens's passionate directness that alarmed the king and his ministers into action.

FIRST SEA BATTLE · VIRGINIA · MORE FROM FRANCE

First Battle of the Virginia Capes

In early March 1781, an opportunity for action finally arose when a storm damaged the British fleet blockading Newport so badly that they had to return to New York for repairs. Admiral Destouches and Rochambeau immediately made plans to sail to Chesapeake Bay, attack Benedict Arnold's ships, deliver 1,000 more soldiers to Lafayette, and do whatever else they could to help in Virginia.

Washington accepted an invitation to come to Newport for the deployment. Preparation of the fleet took so long, however, that the British learned of the plans and had time to make their repairs. The faster British copper-hulled ships actually reached the mouth of the Chesapeake first.

When the French arrived, the two fleets fought for three days off the Virginia Capes. Though neither could claim victory when the British disengaged, the British navy had prevented the French from accomplishing any of their goals.

Lafayette and Von Steuben in Virginia

When Lafayette learned the outcome of the sea battle, he presumed he should return north and started back. Soon after, he received orders to hasten back to the South, and only his leadership overcame his men's angry reluctance.

From late April through May 1781, the Continentals under Lafayette and militia under both Lafayette and von Steuben struggled across Virginia against the much larger British army now led by Cornwallis. The British were voracious in their seizures and destruction of military stores and ironworks, knowing the Patriot forces in the South desperately needed all that could be sent. Ahead of the British, Lafayette had insured that a vast portion of the Patriot munitions in Richmond were secretely hauled far to the west and hidden in the countryside. Lafayette and his men stung and thwarted the British at every opportunity, slowing them so they burned through supplies while accomplishing less than they intended. So too, he ordered many of the British prisoners to be moved beyond British reach. The British themselves, as they had in the Carolinas, helped the Patriots unintentionally. They drove neutral and even Loyalist Virginians to become Patriots through their indiscriminate harshness, theft, and destruction.

Early in June, Cornwallis led his army further and further westward, burning, seizing, and capturing. Under orders to capture Jefferson and leading legislators, Tarleton's infamous light cavalry raced far beyond the main British columns, all the way to Charlottesville, and Jefferson's home, Monticello. However, Tarleton failed to find Jefferson, the hidden stores, or British prisoners. Had they been seized, the results would have been devastating for the Allies. In mid June 1781, in response to orders from General Clinton, Cornwallis turned his army back toward the coast.

Relief from Versailles

On May 7, 1781, after a wait of nine months, Rochambeau's son returned. He brought the dreaded news that his father's second division would never be coming. However, he also had marvelous news: France had given an outright gift of six and one half million *livres*, much of which the young vicomte had brought.

Soon thereafter, a letter from John Laurens arrived, written from France in April. It contained:

> *It is his most Christian Majesty's determination to guarantee a loan of ten millions of livres, to be opened in Holland, in favor of the United States, in addition to the gratuitous gift of six millions granted before my arrival....*

In fact, though no one in America knew it, Louis XVI had taken out a loan in his own name to obtain that money because the Dutch would not extend the Americans any credit.

Surpassing even this, Laurens announced that Admiral de Grasse and a huge fleet had already departed for the Caribbean and the United States with instructions to be of "significant service to the interests of America." The news was electrifying. With naval support, the American Revolution would survive and decisive action could be taken.

King Louis XVI of France

GENERAL PLANNING AND PREPARATION

Wethersfield Plan

Generals Washington and Rochambeau met at Wethersfield, Connecticut on May 21 through May 23, 1781. They decided that with the support of de Grasse's fleet, they would attack either New York City or the Chesapeake as soon as possible. The generals were looking for their best chance for a resounding victory that might help win the war.

Washington still favored New York. The city had been seized brutally and held by the British for so long that it had become a symbol; for the sake of Patriot morale and commitment, it needed to be retaken. Additionally, New York was nearby, familiar terrain while Virginia was well over 400 miles away. The logistical difficulty of two huge armies traversing over 450 miles in the heat of summer was staggering, and the odds of getting there before the British caught on and outstripped them by sea were poor. Washington also had concerns about his army's reaction to the Chesapeake Bay area. Most northern soldiers dreaded the southern heat and diseases. Finally, Washington favored attacking New York because fewer British soldiers occupied the city than normal, and he believed they could be beaten.

Generals' meeting place,
Joseph Webb's house, Wethersfield

Rochambeau strongly preferred attacking the Chesapeake. He believed that without massive naval superiority, New York City was unconquerable. The British in New York, even depleted, had more men than the French and Americans combined plus reputably formidable fortifications. The British navy could maneuver in and out of the harbor, and both men knew that the French ships might not be able to clear the sandbars at Sandy Hook. If the French fleet could not enter the harbor, it would not be able to bombard the enemy.

Ultimately, Admiral de Grasse and factors yet unknown would determine the choice, so the generals decided to position both armies in Philipsburg, New York, an area north of New York City. There, they would examine the enemy fortifications and await word from de Grasse before making the decision.

Rochambeau wrote to de Grasse, making clear how important his help would be. He also urged

the admiral to pick the Chesapeake, and asked him to bring more soldiers, a great deal of money, and cannons of various types with ammunition. Rochambeau entrusted the letter to the captain of a fast, small ship who had to evade the British navy and deliver the letter to the Admiral wherever he was in the Caribbean—immediately.

Six months prior to the Wethersfield meeting, a unified action somewhere had been almost a certainty, so preparations had begun before the meeting. Settling on routes was a joint decision, involving input from Washington, Rochambeau, and Jeremiah Wadsworth, the exemplary American Commissary to the French army and navy in America. At the same time, Wadsworth had started arranging provisions for thousands of men and animals along the route.

The French Army Prepares to March to Philipsburg, New York

As preparations accelerated, everyone knew that some men would have to remain in Newport, but few of the French were willing to stay. At least one duel resulted. By June 10, 1781, the army was ready to move. In some cases, the days before departure were tearful ones because these men had been in the country for almost a year and close ties had developed.

Supplying the March

After leaving behind the units charged with protecting Newport, the sick, and the fleet, 5,300 soldiers began the trip. Approximately 450 of these were officers. Civilian cooks, drivers, and body servants added another 1,300 or more to the march.

Moving en masse required painstaking planning and enormous quantities of almost everything. Some things they took with them, but much had to be delivered where and when needed. The commissary officers were masters of supply. In one single letter to the people of Bolton, Connecticut, Wadsworth inspired with patriotism, lured with price, and threatened with seizure if they would not sell to the army.

All equipment had to be in good shape initially, and spare parts and tools for almost every conceivable repair had to be taken as well. Over 850 horses and 600 oxen were needed for the wagon train, with 500 more horses for the artillery. Officers' mounts may have brought the total to 3,000 animals. Of course, that meant that forage and water would be needed for all of them.

All armies march on their stomachs. These soldiers needed portable ovens, and at least 200 head of cattle (with a reserve of 200 more) and 200 sheep every week, plus feed and water enough to sustain the livestock until they were butchered. At each stopping point, the commissary officers had waiting for them not only provisions for the stock but also other

stores, planned out for what would be needed. For example, in East Hartford, Connecticut, the men drew four days' rations, and in Newtown, Connecticut, 2,520 bushels of corn, 3,161 bushels of oats, huge quantities of wood and straw, and another herd of cattle were waiting for them.

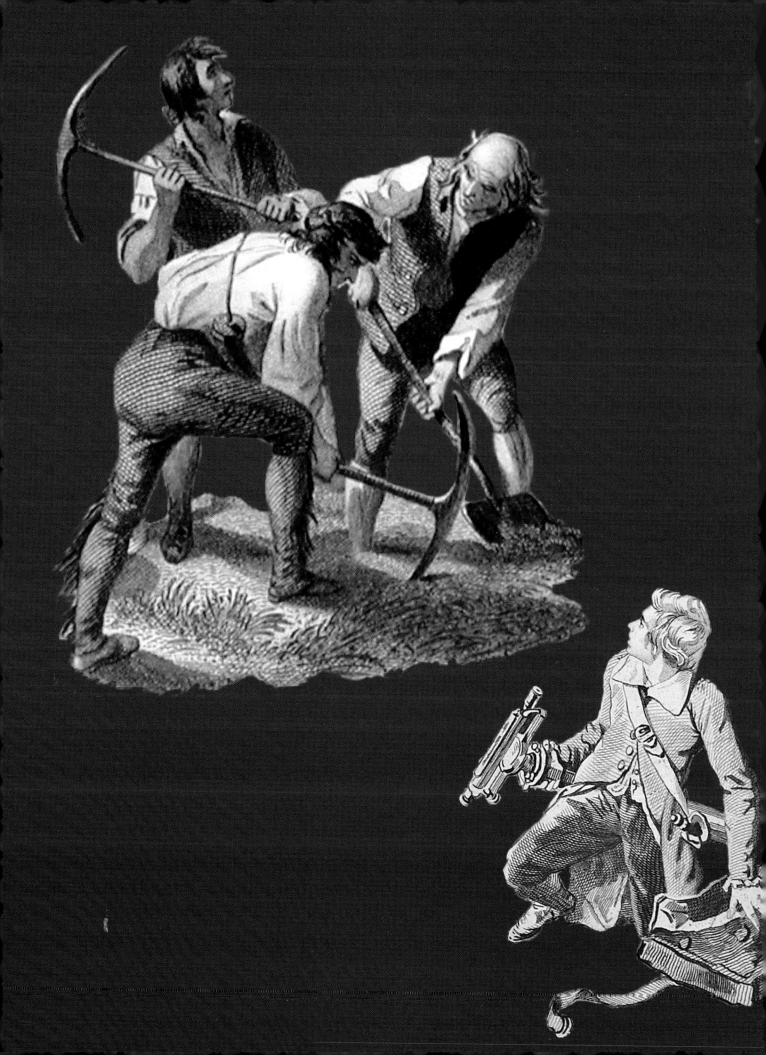

MARCH TO PHILIPSBURG

By Sea to Providence

On June 11, 1781, the French army boarded a motley collection of small vessels in Newport for the passage to Providence. After a day's travel across the bay and up the Providence River, the companies began assembling on land. The process of getting everything and everyone in place required several days. On June 16, replacements arrived to replenish each unit.

That same day Commissary Claude Blanchard and Quartermaster General de Bréville (with staff) headed out on the road the army would take to mark the camps and make sure everything needed was in place. The siege guns and artillerymen had to stay in Newport because the weapons were far too heavy and unwieldy for overland transport.

Order of March

Two days later, on June 18, the French army began its march to New York with Rochambeau leading the first regiment. Each regiment of the main force left Providence a day apart in this order:

- The Bourbonnais Regiment under Comte de Rochambeau departed June 18.
- The Royal Deux-Ponts Regiment under Baron de Vioménil departed June 19.
- The Soissonnais Regiment under Comte de Vioménil departed June 20.
- The Saintonge Regiment under Comte de Custine departed June 21.

Duc de Lauzun's force, Lauzun's Legion, departed June 20, taking a different route altogether, several miles to the south. His men would serve as a screen between the vulnerable columns and possible attack from Long Island Sound, passing through Lebanon, Middletown, Wallingford, Oxford, Ridgefield, and other towns before rejoining the main body.

Anatomy of the Marching Column

Ahead of the forward column of each regiment, a small force filled potholes in the roads, removed obstructions, and marked the turns to keep everyone on course.

Then came the main body of the regiment, often led by drummers and musicians. There was a specific placement in the marching column for everything. Behind the soldiers came carriages and guns, the horse-drawn artillery, ammunition wagons, and forges.

The baggage train was next, with generals' wagons first, then artillery wagons, staff wagons, at least ten regimentals (one wagon per company carrying the company tents and the officers' luggage), a stragglers' wagon, and several hospital wagons. (By journey's end, 227 of the 5,300 fighting men in this force were in hospitals.) Then came wagons for butchers, bread, fodder, a Provost's (military police) wagon, and finally wheelwrights and farriers' (men who took care of horse hooves) wagons. Within the convoy were 230 four-oxen or six-oxen wagon teams and 20 four-horse teams for the wagons of the general staff, as well. Rochambeau also hired 239 wagoneers and cooks for the march.

No one traveled light. In addition to equipment and horses, officers were expected to have and provide for servants. Lieutenants hired at least one or two, and generals had ten or more. These domestics and horses added 500 to 1,000 people and about 1,500 horses to the column. Everything worn or carried, even in summer, was heavy. The common soldiers wore uniforms consisting of long wool underwear, breeches, a long-sleeved coat worn buttoned, coverings for the lower legs and upper part of their shoes. Each man carried about 60 pounds of gear in addition to their ten-pound muskets.

A Typical Day on the March

To avoid the worst heat of the day, reveille (a bugle call) woke the men at two in the morning, and by four in the morning they were heading out in a relaxed order. As soon as the musicians struck the marching cadence, they tightened their columns, following the drums and music through the dark. By midday, having covered twelve to fifteen miles, the soldiers would reach the next bivouac (camp ground). The pace, less than two miles an hour, was set primarily by the oxen-drawn wagons, but fit men

could keep this up for days in a row. At each encampment they usually found fresh water, cattle to be butchered, and other provisions. They would make camp, pitching tents, digging latrines, and setting up cooking fires. The high-ranking officers usually stayed in taverns, and the company officers shared

two-man tents with or near their men. Common soldiers slept several to a tent. Setting up camp was a swift process. Afterwards, small groups of men would receive and cook their daily rations, and then relax or visit. It was the first time most people along the routes had ever met a Frenchman, so the opportunity to make a good impression was important and soldiers used it well.

Even though everyone was tired by the end of each day's march, musicians played as they approached their campsites. The marching music, the exotic and exciting sights, and the opportunity to sell their surplus goods for hard coin drew Americans to them. Whenever possible, the soldiers enjoyed dancing with local beauties to the music of the regimental band. One soldier, Georg Daniel Flohr of the Royal-Deux Pont, recorded as part of his journal:

...marched 12 miles to Farmington, a little town. As soon as we had set up our camp there and the

Turkish Music could be heard playing prettily, such a large number of inhabitants assembled there that one was surprised and had to wonder where all these people were coming from since we had encountered very few houses along our way during the daytime. This coming together of inhabitants continued to happen every day. As soon as we reached another camp we were immediately surrounded by Americans.

Among them one saw very few male persons however but only women folk: if one saw a man among them it was unfailingly an old man or a cripple because all men folk from their 14th until their 60th year had to join the colors. Because of this there was a great dearth of men there. Almost everyone there nearly perished since the English treated them very badly at the time. But there was no lack of women folk....

Flohr wrote this about their overnight stop at Southington, Connecticut:

On the 28th (i.e., 27th) we marched 13 miles to Barnes' Tavern, an inn along the road. We set up our camp very close to it. We again had very numerous visits from the American maidens who circled the camp on horseback and who appeared just like English horsemen. This afternoon our …generals gave a ball on the open field in front of our camp and invited the American maidens to it. This lasted into the dark night. All joy could be seen there what with dancing and singing as well with the soldiers as with the officers who had fun with the English girls. After that we went to sleep in our tents, but the girls went home all sad.

The conditions of the road varied from good to almost impassable. Though the year in Newport had familiarized the French somewhat with American culture, the road to New York

took them into regions and among people more different still. During the first many days of the march, despite stifling heat, the fertile, beautiful land and gracious reception by every community enchanted them. They were equally struck by the absence of beggars and by the fact that even the poorest people were rich compared to the poor of France. Traveling westward through Plainfield,

Windham, Bolton, East Hartford (where they rested an extra night), Farmington, Southington, and Breakneck (now Middlebury/Waterbury), the army felt unthreatened. They posted sentries at night, but only as a matter of good military procedure.

Into Tory Country

However, as they neared Newtown, Connecticut (about 80 miles northeast of the British headquarters in New York City), they entered disputed territory, and much changed. Farmland was scarred or abandoned, and homes lay in ruin. Inhabitants were visibly poorer. Loyalist militiamen waged guerrilla warfare against the French, particularly at night, and then faded back into civilian life. In response, sentries and outriders were increased day and night. There was no way to distinguish a friendly stranger from one only pretending to be, so distrust and tension replaced the mental ease to which the soldiers had become accustomed. By the time they reached Newtown, the men had endured eleven scorching marches, the last under constant threat of attack.

In Newtown, the weary men rested for a desperately needed extra night, so the divisions overlapped for a few hours.

At about this time, Washington called upon the French to help attack a Loyalist force at Morrisania (now South Bronx). They responded immediately. This was their first opportunity to show the Americans what they could do in battle, and the soldiers wanted to impress. In two strenuous days, the furthest troops involved covered nearly 45 miles, an extraordinary feat, arriving on time in Bedford, New York, the rally site. The condition of the town shocked and appalled the French army. They had witnessed the ravages of war during the past few days, but this area had been a battle zone for three years by the summer of 1781. Most Bedford homes had been gutted or burned to the ground.

The French army executed its orders brilliantly. Then they assembled 13 miles north at North Castle (now Mount Kisco), New York on July 4–5. That town, too, had been devastated. While the army rested, Washington and Rochambeau conferred.

Though the French were normally punctilious about paying for their provisions and maintaining good relations with locals, they would do what they had to do. Louis Alexandre Berthier wrote that he had been sent ahead on July 3 with an escort to obtain wagons at the halfway point for the sick and exhausted. "Since we were now on the edge of enemy territory, I was ordered to seize by force whatever was not yielded voluntarily. Using both methods, I obtained everything I needed."

Early the third morning at North Castle, Rochambeau's forces marched southwest toward Philipsburg, a small town in the highlands on the east bank of the Hudson. It was approximately 20 miles north of the British High Command in Manhattan. Clermont-Crèvecoer described the experience:

> *The roads were so bad that the last division of artillery, to which I was attached, did not arrive in camp until an hour after midnight. The troops had been on the road since three o'clock the morning without anything to eat. They found nothing to drink on the way. Casting your eyes over the countryside, you felt very sad, for it revealed all the horrors and cruelty of the English in burned woodlands, destroyed houses, and fallow fields deserted by the owners. It is impossible to be more uncomfortable than we were that day; more than 400 soldiers dropped from fatigue, and it was only by frequent halts and much care that we brought everyone into camp.*

 NEWPORT 2   PROVIDENCE 3

 PLAINFIELD 4   WINDHAM 5   BOLTON 6   EAST HARTFORD 7

 FARMINGTON 10   SOUTHINGTON 11   BREAKNECK 12
(MIDDLELEBURY/WATERBURY)

 NEWTOWN 13   BEDFORD 14

 NORTH CASTLE (MT. KISKO) 15   LEBANON 16   MIDDLETOWN 17

 WALLINGSFORD 18   OXFORD 19   RIDGEFIELD 20

IMPRESSIONS OF THE ALLIES

The French Army at Philipsburg, New York

The French were encamped near Philipsburg by July 6, 1781, two weeks after they had left Newport. In that time they had covered over 200 miles, taken time out for a battle, protected themselves from attack day and night, and endeared themselves to countless Americans by their exemplary behavior. With justification Lauzun boasted,

> *The French army marched through America in perfect order and with perfect discipline, setting an example which neither the English nor the American army had ever furnished.*

The Philipsburg encampment and its river-edge gun emplacements protected the eastern Hudson River shore between Tarrytown and Dobbs Ferry. The area closest to the Hudson was reserved for the Americans, so the French army arranged itself on the broad area just east of the Americans.

Armand Louis de Gontaut, duc de Lauzun

Continental Army at Philipsburg, New York

One day later, Washington's 4,000 Continentals arrived from New York and New Jersey winter camps. These men were the hardship-thinned, loyal diehards, the battle-honed core of the Northern army. Though poorly outfitted, they were outstanding soldiers. Within a day their camp was completed, a stone's throw from the French, separated only by a small stream. The commanders on both sides had grave concerns about the sudden proximity of the two armies. In manners, customs, and beliefs as well as language, Americans and Frenchmen were vastly different. The French army had been afforded months to acclimate to American ways, but the Americans had had little or no exposure to the French. Even though only French officers would lead French soldiers, and only American officers would lead Americans, it was essential that the two groups maintained good relations. At a soldier-to-soldier level, could they? Fortunately discipline on both sides was tight and most soldiers behaved well.

The very next day, July 8, Rochambeau's army presented a review. Officially the show was intended for French Ambassador La Luzerne, who was there for the day, but the American troops could not help being impressed by the stunning uniforms and flawless drill. A day later the Americans returned the honor. Clermont-Crèvecoeur recorded his impression:

> *I went to the American camp, which contained approximately 4,000 men. In beholding this army I was struck, not by its smart appearance, but by its destitution: the men were without uniforms and covered with rags; most of them were barefoot. They were of all sizes, down to children who could not have been over fourteen. There were many negroes, mulattoes, etc. I realized that the soldiers I was seeing were the elite of the country and...actually very good troops, well schooled in their profession. We had nothing but praise for them later; Marie François, baron Cromot du Bourg, said the Continental Army seemed*

"to be in as good order as possible for an army composed of men without uniforms and with narrow resources."

Some of the Americans actually did have uniforms, and among these were the Rhode Island Regiment, three quarters of whom were Blacks. About the Americans, particularly about the Rhode Island unit under the command of Lieutenant Colonel Jeremiah Olney, Baron von Closen said:

> *I had a chance to see the American army, man for man. It was really painful to see these brave men, almost naked with only some trousers and little linen jackets, most of them without stockings, but, would you believe it? Very cheerful and healthy in appearance. A quarter of them were negroes, merry, confident, and sturdy.... Three quarters of the Rhode Island regiment consists of negroes, and that regiment is the most neatly dressed, the best under arms, and the most precise in its maneuvers.*

Rochambeau was so moved by the state of the Americans that he immediately wrote to the French ministers, urging them to forward generous amounts of money as soon as possible. He wrote not only of his high expenses but also the fact that his "neighbors lack everything...."

There were personal misunderstandings and resentments from time to time, but the good will was real. Over time men on both sides moved from mutual curiosity, bafflement and even amazement to respect, and in some cases true friendship.

For the next month as they waited for word from Admiral de Grasse, the two high generals reconnoitered, tested the enemy, and planned. Their officers and soldiers defended the camp, skirmished occasionally, and prepared. For a time Washington held to his hope of retaking New York, and more than one letter dealing with the subject was captured and seen by the British commander, General Henry Clinton.

BRITISH FORCES

WASHINGTON'S HEADQUARTER'S 8

WASHINGTON'S CAMP 1

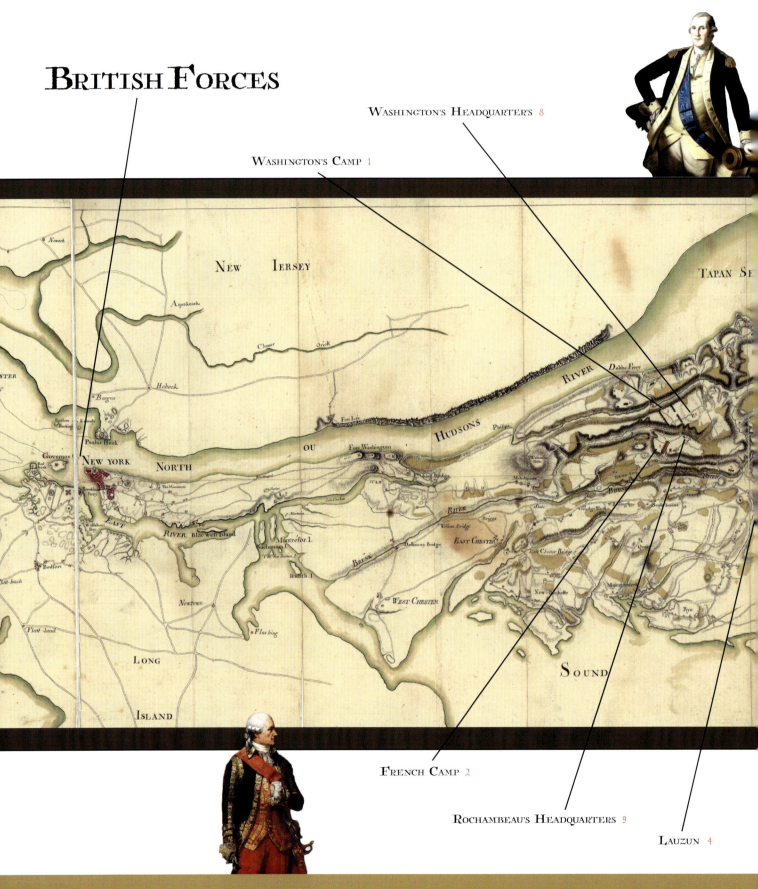

FRENCH CAMP 2

ROCHAMBEAU'S HEADQUARTERS 9

LAUZUN 4

DECISION TIME

British Response to the Allied Army at Their Door

The British army in New York never attacked in force. Washington and Rochambeau were amazed, but General Clinton had his reasons. He believed the French would be gone in a year and that as long as he did not lose beforehand, the Americans would eagerly accept British terms once they were abandoned. Also, based on captured letters and his spies' reports, Clinton was certain a massive attack on the city was coming. He strengthened his defenses and stayed within them. He was so focused on New York that in June he had ordered Cornwallis to transfer 2,000 men to the Virginia coast so that they could be returned to New York.

In Virginia

In early June, Cornwallis had turned his army toward the coast. Dogged by Lafayette every step of the way, Cornwallis's army traversed the Virginia peninsula. For a number of weeks, Tarleton's Legion operated independently. They used their lightning strike capability to catch Virginia civilians unaware and to forcefully steal many of the state's finest horses. By late August, Tarleton and the horses had rejoined Cornwallis. They were awaiting ships in camps on both sides of the York River in Yorktown and Gloucester. With their backs to the wide river and significantly outnumbering their foe, the British began building fortifications without any great sense of alarm. Meanwhile, Lafayette did all he could with limited troops to keep the enemy from decamping.

Banastre Tarleton

Momentous Decision

On August 14, 1781, aware that Cornwallis was fortifying Yorktown, Washington learned that Admiral de Grasse was on his way to the Chesapeake with at least 25 ships of war, 3,000 Caribbean infantrymen, and more. However, the ships and soldiers could only stay until October 15. Therefore, the Allies had to get themselves to Virginia, and every hour would count. Success would hinge on several factors:

- Admiral de Grasse's fleet arriving unscathed all the way from the West Indies and then controlling the Chesapeake sea-lanes and rivers
- Cornwallis's army remaining at Yorktown
- General Clinton's army and navy remaining in New York

- Admiral de Barras's fleet arriving with siege guns, ammunition, artillerymen and provisions from Newport
- the American and French armies making it to Yorktown in force, with all equipment and in good health over hundreds of miles within weeks

All of this had to happen with pinpoint timing, without any effective way to communicate.

Washington wrote Lafayette the very next day, ordering him to keep Cornwallis at Yorktown, without divulging anything more. He also wrote a second letter in code that explained everything, and General Duportail was given the mission to deliver it in person to both Admiral de Grasse and Lafayette.

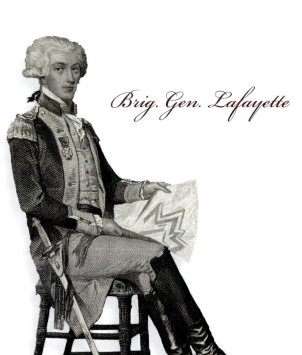

Brig. Gen. Lafayette

General Duportail

Admiral de Grasse

MISDIRECTION

Last Minute Preparations

Also on August 14, Washington gave General William Heath two critical tasks. He had to convince the British that the remaining Continental army was massive and that the full land and sea attack on New York City was imminent. Second, he must protect the whole Hudson Highland, including West Point, though only a skeleton force of 2,500 men would remain. General Heath's Continentals would be outnumbered four to one by the British, a fact he had to keep the enemy from discovering.

Without a moment to lose, the command staff finalized all the routes, stopping points, and supplies for the march, all under tight security. Then they positioned units to completely block the west side of the Hudson River for miles for the next months, to deter British intelligence and pursuit. In the same few days, company officers readied their men to depart.

Counterintelligence

Misdirecting Clinton as long as possible was essential. Washington knew spies would learn whatever his men knew, so he and Rochambeau blatantly misled almost everyone even as the men readied to march.

To reinforce the threat of an impending attack on New York, rafts to carry men to Staten Island were built, and soldiers repaired roads on attack routes. A bakery big enough to bake for thousands went up in New Jersey close to Staten Island, and food was stockpiled for delivery to local depots. Misleading dispatches intentionally sent along routes patrolled by British soldiers were seized. With all this evidence and the actual letters from Washington that had been captured earlier, Clinton was given every reason to believe the attack on New York would come soon.

Women often served as spies because they traveled commonly and freely into camps. The deposition of a British spymaster reveals how such spies became the unwitting carriers of false information back to the British. During the second week of August 1781, "Miss Jenny" made her way into the French camp, pretending to look for her father. After discovery, she was interrogated for several days by Rochambeau and Washington and then allowed to leave, suffering nothing worse than having her hair cut short to mark her as a spy. During her time there, Washington and Rochambeau made sure she was exposed to exactly what they wanted her to see and hear.

The following is an excerpt from the deposition of Baron Ottendorf after his spy, "Miss Jenny" returned from the French camp near Philipsburg.

...then (for her) to be set on a horse with neither bonnet nor hair covering, sitting on a cloak between two soldiers and (for her) to be led in this manner outside of the lines with the order not to return unless she wants to run the risk of being severely punished. She says that everything is ready with them for advancing and that the general opinion is that he (Washington) wants to come and attack in two places as soon as their fleet arrives. She saw your Jaegers arrive yesterday, around 4 or 5. They were not retained; they were sent immediately to Philadelphia. When these Jaegers arrived at Washington's quarters, he had them given something to drink and eat, informing them that soon all of your people will come, and that in a short while he will be in York.

TWO ARMIES IN JERSEY

March to Philadelphia

In just three nonstop days, the first units began crossing the Hudson River at Dobbs Ferry. Soon after, the French and other American units were also crossing at King's Ferry. The Continental Army heading southward included 2,500 soldiers, and the French Army totaled 5,350 at this time. Simultaneously, General Hazen's Regiment moved down the coast opposite Staten Island and made camp, making sure they were seen. By August 26, 1781, the Allied forces had all crossed the Hudson and disappeared from view, and because of Hazen's men, an attack on New York now looked certain. The challenges of moving this joint army were staggering. Unlike the French trip from Rhode Island, preparations were completed on the fly. Roads were terrible in places, and bridges had to be repaired or even built ahead of the oncoming armies. Loyalist bands were often a danger in the first days, and the vulnerable columns and wagons stretched for miles. Cattle were driven ahead of the army and slaughtered before the men arrived. Soldiers were rising by half past two

each morning, marching within ninety minutes, camping by early afternoon, and drawing their day's rations soon after.

Provisions Per Soldier Authorized by Congress November 4, 1775

One pound of bread or flour per day

Half a pound of beef and half a pound of pork, & if pork cannot be had, One pound and a quarter of beef per day; and one day in seven they shall have one pound and one quarter of salt fish

One pint of milk per day, when it's to be had

One quart of good spruce or malt beer or cider per day

One gill of peas or beans, or other vegetables equivalent per week

Six ounces of good butter per week

One pound of good common soap for six men per week

Half a pint of vinegar per week per man, if it can be had

Half a pint of rice or 1 pint of Indian meal per man per week

A marching soldier needs a great deal of food; two armies needed unbelievable quantities. As American units traveled from Paramus, Chatham, Springfield, New Brunswick, Kingston, and Princeton, they raised dust "like smothering snow." To ease the burden on any given area, travel faster, and support the myth that they were attacking New York, the army, especially the Continentals, often divided and took several different routes for portions of the march. A day behind them, the French traveled through Whippany, Morristown, Bullion's Tavern (Liberty Corner) and Somerset Courthouse (Millstone), sometimes entertaining the townspeople with music as they passed. The armies could not have sustained that pace or themselves without the good will of the locals. Nonetheless, so much was needed that sometimes Americans, who had only paper money, could not find willing sellers on short notice. When that happened, the soldiers took what they needed, leaving angry owners with IOUs. The French had better luck because they had silver. Fortunately, the further the armies traveled, the easier procurement became; states and local communities had time to prepare and wanted to do so.

Like clockwork, the men rose, ate, broke

camp, marched, made camp, ate, socialized if they could, rested, slept, and began again, consuming the miles. It was not until August 31, as the columns turned westward toward Trenton, that soldiers concluded they were heading for Virginia. When Clinton heard of the turn, he finally started wondering if New York really was the target.

French Impressions

As they traveled, the French were charmed by what they saw. Baron von Closen wrote:

> *The Jerseys where we are now—beautiful country!—abound in all kinds of produce.... The inhabitants...have kept it neat.... It is a land of milk and honey with game, fish, vegetables, poultry, etc. After leaving New York State, where misery is written on the brows of the inhabitants, the affluence of the state of the Jerseys seems to be much greater.*

The comfort in which the general population lived compared to the ragged condition of most American soldiers was the opposite of reality in Europe. The French soldiers had great sympathy for their American brothers-in-arms, yet had much to ponder in the face of widespread civilian prosperity and opportunity.

News from de Barras

As the armies traveled south through New Jersey, a messenger brought word that Admiral de Barras had sailed from Newport with the siege guns to join de Grasse at the Chesapeake. This was an enormous relief. As the senior naval officer, de Barras could have refused. His involvement meant that if his ships arrived intact, the combined fleet would be larger than that of the British, and the weapons essential for the siege (encirclement and sustained attack) of Yorktown would be there. Like almost everything else about their mission, the commanders kept this news secret.

DOBBS FERRY 25   KING'S FERRY 24   STATEN ISLAND 27   PARAMUS 28

CHATHAM 29   SPRINGFIELD 30   PRINCETON 35   WHIPPANY 31

MORRISTOWN 32   BULLION'S TAVERN 33   SOMERSET COURTHOUSE 34
(LIBERTY CORNER)   (MILLSTONE)

Philadelphia Interlude

Washington and Rochambeau rode ahead to Philadelphia, arriving in the early afternoon of August 30, 1781. For three days they met formally and informally with congressmen, the French Ambassador, and other Patriot leaders.

On September 1, worrisome news arrived. British Admiral Hood had sailed south from New York with about twenty fighting ships. Washington and Rochambeau feared for Admiral de Barras who was believed to be en route from Newport with a dozen fighting ships plus transports.

Both the French army and the first division of the Continental army laboriously crossed the Delaware River at Trenton by ferry and sailboat, and then traveled the 35 miles to Philadelphia. When American soldiers marched through Philadelphia on the scorching afternoon of September 2, their two-mile long line tromped stonily past the waving crowds in a thick cloud of choking dust. The men were a shocking sight to many Philadelphians who had never realized how ragged their army was. The soldiers were hot and angry, knew they were shabby, and were in no mood for a showy parade. Unpaid for a very long time, they simmered with resentment over the upcoming trek to the "pestilential South."

Two days later, the French arrival was far different. They had taken the time to groom themselves and change into their best uniforms shortly before arriving, and their impact was electrifying. As one officer wrote, "The arrival of the French troops…was in the nature of a triumph." The French were just as delighted and amazed by Philadelphia. People, commerce, egalitarian attitudes, fashions, wonderful schools, pursuit of science, religious tolerance, and even Philadelphians' frank pursuit of wealth all introduced a new appreciation of America to the men of France. This was indeed a new world.

Philadelphia

On September 4, the same day that French soldiers performed a formal review, almost 1,600 Continentals and more than 500 horses and oxen left their camps around Chester, Pennsylvania and marched through Wilmington, Delaware, bedding down just beyond the city. Wilmington, the largest town in the state, only had 1,200 inhabitants, so the soldiers more than matched them in numbers and need for food. The next day, this column trekked through Christiana, Delaware and from there to Head of Elk (now Elkton), Maryland, a port town at the northern shore of the great Chesapeake Bay.

Hazen's Regiment Rejoins the March

Hazen's Regiment had stayed behind near New York City to guard the rear and confuse the British while Washington and Rochambeau's columns had moved through New Jersey. At great risk to themselves, they had succeeded; their disception of the British had bought the time the Allies had needed to get well away. On August 28, 1781, Hazen's men had left their location near New York. They sped mostly by water to Christiana Bridge, where they rejoined the rest of the Continentals.

Soldier serving in Hazen's Regiment

EVENTS IN THE CHESAPEAKE · TIMELY LOAN · MOUNT VERNON

Admiral de Grasse Arrives

On September 5, Rochambeau and his staff were stunned to see a man dressed like their Commander-in-Chief jumping up and down on a river landing, waving excitedly, barely able to contain himself. Surely the man could not possibly be Washington, whose composure was legendary. Yet it was! As Comte de Deux-Ponts put it, "a child whose wishes had been satisfied could not have expressed a more lively expression of pleasure." Washington rushed up to Rochambeau and hugged him, exclaiming again and again "He's here! He's here!" Word had come that Admiral de Grasse's entire fleet had arrived safely in the Chesapeake on August 30, and had already delivered the 3,000 soldiers to Lafayette! From the moment this news spread, the soldiers spoke of Cornwallis as though he were already their captive.

Rochambeau and his army left Chester for Head of Elk, Maryland on September 6, one day after the Americans. At each stop, the Patriot army was viewed both with greater trust and greater dread than the French who followed—more trust simply because they were American; greater dread because they could not pay well or at all for the supplies they required, while the French paid in silver coin.

A Timely Loan

Another great American worry was laid to rest before departure from Head of Elk when Rochambeau loaned the Americans $26,000 to pay soldiers some of their past due wages. Continental private Plumb Martin echoed the stunned reaction of every enlistee when he wrote,

We each of us received a MONTH'S PAY, in specie, borrowed…from the French army. This was the first that could be called money [coins], which we had received as wages since the year 1776, or that we ever did receive till the close of the war, or indeed, ever after, as wages.

This unprecedented act bolstered morale tremendously.

From Head of Elk, Maryland to the James River in Virginia

The plan had been for the army to sail from Head of Elk to near Yorktown, but British raiding parties had taken or destroyed most of the large vessels. With help from men from Maryland's eastern shore, every small boat that could be pressed into service began loading most of the American army, 1,200 French troops, and masses of supplies for the trip to Baltimore. The rest would trek overland. On September 8, Washington, accompanied by some staff, guards, and servants, galloped ahead to Baltimore to seek transport from there to near Yorktown for everyone. Rochambeau and some of his staff followed as the first columns traveling by land pulled out. Three days later, the boats carrying soldiers and military goods released their moorings.

French soldiers, the wagon train, and heavy equipment moved forward at an average speed of three miles an hour, a punishing pace to keep up for hours even on level roads. Approximately 2,500 men, divided into two sections, traveled one day apart. Day after day, they marched through heat and storms over land and trails described as "diabolic," "frightful," and "abominable." The columns snaked for miles past people who would talk about them for the rest of their lives.

Mount Vernon Interlude

On the morning of September 9, after accomplishing all he could in Baltimore, Washington and one of his staff rode 50 miles to Mount Vernon at such speed that they arrived before dark. Martha, Washington's "dearest Patsy," was waiting. There was light enough for the general to gaze over the Potomac from the veranda for the first time in six years. By racing, Washington had

bought them precious time before Rochambeau and both generals' staffs arrived for two days of respite and serious planning. For the first time, he saw his newly renovated home and his four grandchildren, all of whom had been born during the war years. Even those hours were filled with a multitude of tasks, all necessary if roads and provisions were to be ready for the coming army.

Martha, in her own sphere, was as busy as he.

By mealtime the next day, Washington's staff joined them, and by that evening Rochambeau and his staff had arrived as well. Mount Vernon was a golden setting for their unending work. Staff and other riders were constantly coming and going, carrying essential messages.

The French Fleet Is Missing!

After three nights, Washington and his party rode south. On the way, they met a messenger bound for Congress carrying news that a week earlier de Grasse's fleet had sailed out to open sea to engage the British and had not been sighted since. If he had been defeated, their planned attack of Yorktown would be all but hopeless.

That same day, troop transports from Head of Elk arrived in Baltimore, and they too learned the grave news about de Grasse. Washington immediately sent orders for the units to wait in place until the outcome of the naval battle was known. However, units of soldiers continued moving southward until Washington's order reached them. Some left from Baltimore and Fell's Point, while others, primarily the Bourbonnais Regiment under Vioménil, marched overland.

Admiral de Grasse sails out of Cap-Français

Twenty-eight ships of the line, seven frigates and two cutters

heading for Yorktown

Ville de Paris

The flagship of Admiral de Grasse

and paid for by the people of Paris

DE GRASSE'S BRILLIANCE · TAKING WILLIAMSBURG · GENERALS ARRIVE

Voyage of Admiral de Grasse to the Chesapeake

The naval battle that worried everyone had been expected. Its outcome could decide whether success against Cornwallis was possible or completely beyond reach. Back in mid-July in Hispaniola (present day Haiti), Admiral de Grasse had read the letters from Washington and Rochambeau about the great need of his expertise, navy, funds, military supplies, equipment and soldiers. He had immediately sent word that he would meet them at the Chesapeake and readied his fleet.

His captains and their crews were fully set in a matter of days. De Grasse found the needed French soldiers by borrowing them, staking his career on returning these 3,400 men in time for a planned Caribbean action. The money, 2 million *livres* (6 million today), was donated by the ladies of Havana. He also wrote Admiral de Barras, asking for his help, stressing the importance of this battle and the critical part de Barras would play.

On August 5, de Grasse's fleet sailed from Hispaniola, an impressive sight: 28 ships of the line, 7 frigates, and 2 cutters. Its flagship, *Ville de Paris,* was a 110-gun three-deck fighting ship paid for by the people of Paris. She was not just the largest ship in the navy; she was exotic. The crew had even adorned her with potted plants to create a lush, floating garden. To elude the British, de Grasse's ships dashed to America through dangerous, usually avoided waters and hugged the coast rather than follow the more direct and safer open sea route.

Admiral Hood in Pursuit

Admiral de Grasse had chosen his route well. Five days after the French departure, British Rear Admiral Hood and his 14 faster warships sailed from Antigua, a British held Caribbean island, northward toward the Chesapeake. Hood did not know his prey's size, location, or even destination. He took the open sea route, expecting to overtake the enemy, and reached the Chesapeake on August 25 to find it empty. Thinking the French had gone to New York, Hood raced north, hoping the battle had not already ended. On August 28, the sight of

British ships sitting peacefully at anchor inside the New York harbor astounded him.

He found General Clinton and Admiral of the Fleet Graves comfortably chatting when he burst into headquarters. Though far beneath them in rank, Hood galvanized the senior officers, and orders were given for fast repairs and departure. That very night they learned that de Barras's squadron had left Newport. They concluded that unless they dealt with the French navy immediately, a coordinated land and sea attack on New York would result. They were also aware that they needed to get to Cornwallis, still waiting at Yorktown.

De Grasse Enters the Chesapeake

On August 28, 1781, the day Hood arrived in New York, de Grasse's fleet passed between the capes into the Chesapeake. The fleet dropped anchor in Lynnhaven Bay, below the mouths of the James and York Rivers, and began transporting military goods and men up the James. Cornwallis's only response was to send notification northward to Clinton and to continue building the fortifications Clinton had demanded.

Admiral de Grasse was upset that the Allied Armies had not yet arrived. He seriously considered attacking Cornwallis without them, but Lafayette urged him to wait. Within days, General Duportail arrived with Washington's letter, which completely changed the crusty admiral's frame of mind.

Admiral de Grasse

General Duportail

Tightening the Noose

After midnight of September 2, Lafayette's Continentals welcomed more than 3,300 French soldiers as they disembarked near Jamestown and reported for duty. Anthony Wayne said that these French soldiers from Hispaniola were "the finest and best made body of men [he] ever beheld," and with their arrival, the Allies' land force on the Virginia penisula increased to 5,500 regulars and 3,000 militia.

With de Grasse's ships sealing the coast and rivers and enough men to cover major avenues of land escape, the Allies were finally strong enough to move into Williamsburg on September 4.

The next day, however, the waterways were wide open again, and the fleet was gone! The combined British fleet had arrived, the French fleet had sailed out to engage, and all had disappeared over the horizon. In the navy's absence, Lafayette's men worked overtime to prepare the ravaged town to receive the Allied Armies while holding the British in place.

Washington and Rochambeau Arrive in Williamsburg

On September 14, Washington and Rochambeau arrived in Williamsburg at last. When Lafayette saw his beloved commander, he galloped up, threw himself from his horse, and hugged Washington, plastering kisses on his cheeks to the astonishment and amusement of those who witnessed it. The general did not seem to mind a bit.

The day was filled with military formalities, but ended with still no word from the absent de Grasse. Everyone feared the worst.

NEW YORK CITY 26   CAPE HENRY 49   CAPE CHARLES 50

LYNNHAVEN BAY 51   WILLIAMSBURG 46

British ships are spotted heading full speed toward the Chesapeake!

Second Battle of the Capes

As they worried in Williamsburg that night, the danger had really just ended.

About ten o'clock in the morning on September 5, a French scouting vessel reported white sails on the horizon. British Admirals Graves and Hood with 19 ships of the line, a 50-gun ship, and support ships were headed full speed toward the mouth of the bay. The British fleet was armed with 1,410 cannons.

Though handicapped by wind, by tide, and by the fact that key officers and crew were ashore, de Grasse knew their best chance lay with getting out of the bay before the enemy arrived. He ordered 24 warships carrying 1,794 guns to cut their anchor lines, and they

De Grasse immediately sets out for the open sea to face the British!

The French and the English engaage in a decisive battle ❧

BATTLE OF

THE CAPES

Without a full crew, the fleet emerged into open sea slowly and awkwardly. Inexplicably, the Royal Navy did not attack then; it was nearly four o'clock in the afternoon when the battle began. In a single hour of fighting, 240 French and 336 British sailors were killed or seriously injured, and ships of both fleets had been hit. The battle ended when the British fled, though the French fleet pursued until dark, and stayed close all night long.

The British fleet had taken very heavy damage, but lack of wind prevented the French from pressing the battle for two days. Both navies used the time to repair all they could. On the third day, September 8, a wind rose that favored the British, so Graves ordered a full assault. In response, the French fleet reversed direction in place and counterattacked. Graves's fleet fled, and the French chased them into the night again.

During the night, the British slipped away, and the French sailed at top speed back to the Chesapeake, fearing that the enemy would be heading there. In fact, Graves refused Hood's urging to race back to save Cornwallis, and the British fleet continued southward. On September 11, the French reentered the Chesapeake to discover that de Barras too was there, with all hands and cargo unharmed. Their combined fleet now had superiority.

The British fleet did limp back to the Chesapeake, arriving September 13. Seeing the combined French fleet, they continued on to New York. Hood was furious and heartsick to have failed Cornwallis. Graves was embarrassed, soothing himself with belief that the coming attack would be against New York, so they could return to Yorktown later. The reality was, however, that Graves had abandoned Cornwallis and his men.

Washington, Rochambeau and de Grasse

After midnight on their first night in Williamsburg, Washington and Rochambeau learned that de Grasse was back victorious and de Barras had arrived! Relief and optimism spread like a comforting blanket through the night, and in the morning, Washington sent dispatch riders north with the good news and orders.

With the fleet again guarding the waterways, the Allies unloaded siege materials and prepared for action. General von Steuben trained the men for siege, and their battlefield responses became coordinated and instantaneous. Cornwallis, alarmed about his position, wrote Clinton on September 17, "This place is in no state of defense. If you cannot relieve me very soon, you must be prepared to hear the worst...."

Washington and Rochambeau needed to plan with de Grasse on the *Ville de Paris*.

The ship was anchored in Lynnhaven Bay near the mouth of the Chesapeake, sixty miles from Williamsburg. The generals and select staff officers sailed all night, and in the morning they found themselves surrounded by massive French ships of the line, an awe-inspiring first for the Americans.

When they were piped aboard, Admiral de Grasse, a bear of a man, stepped forward and embraced Washington, roaring enthusiastically, "*Mon cher petit général! (My dear little general!)*" Laughter lit the deck, a good start. Though de Grasse was at times less than silken-mannered during their conversation, he was ultimately a magnificent partner, agreeing to participate generously in the upcoming weeks.

The meeting came at a price. That evening, after the generals were again on the small vessel that had brought them, they battled a violent storm that prevented headway for three days and nights. Finally, Rochambeau and Washington were rowed tight to shore for thirty miles and then rode borrowed horses the rest of the way to Williamsburg, arriving on September 22.

*British fireship explodes
on the water!*

GLOUCESTER · FIRE ON THE WATER · LOCKDOWN

The Problem of Gloucester

The fortified base on Gloucester Point immediately across the York River from Yorktown was a potential British escape and supply route that needed to be closed. British troops regularly executed brutal raids on that side of the river, overwhelming the American militia that was trying to contain them. Only crack troops in sufficient numbers could realistically hope to succeed. The brash and fierce Lauzun's Legion leapt at the assignment.

Fire on the Water

Cornwallis had begun searching for ways out of the trap in which he found himself. If the three French ships blocking the mouth of the York River could be removed, escape into the Carolinas might be possible. Just before midnight on September 22, the same day Washington and Rochambeau returned from the meeting with de Grasse, 5 fireships, manned by steel-nerved British crewmen silently raced downstream, propelled by wind and the ebb tide current. Each ship was full of tarred wood ready for the match. As the sailors aboard spied the French ships anchored ahead and thought they were about to succeed, one fireship exploded prematurely. From that moment all went wrong for the attackers. Cries went up on the targeted ships, and their crews raced to stations. With astounding speed, the French ships were fleeing while firing at the oncoming enemy. The fireships ignited, blazing to the tops of their masts, but no French ships were damaged because they had been forewarned. With that failure, Cornwallis gave up on a downstream water escape.

Sealing Yorktown on Land

Before dawn on September 28, the Allies, now 18,000 strong, gathered in formation. At daybreak they began marching down the sandy road from Williamsburg to Yorktown. Claude Blanchard and a small squad stayed behind to protect the stores and tend the 300 sick and injured in the hospital set up in the College of William and Mary.

Among the troops moving down the road was one malaria-ridden escapee from Blanchard's field hospital, the Marquis de Saint-Simon, commander of the Caribbean regiments brought by Admiral de Grasse. He refused to remain behind, so he led from a litter.

The men expected to be attacked, but the killer on the road was not the British—they never contested an inch of it. It was the heat, so severe that some hardened soldiers just dropped dead, and many more were incapacitated. The once beautiful land they traversed was a shattered waste, populated only by ghosts.

During the long noon rest, Washington's latest order was read: if attacked, the Allies were to use bayonets. Given the emotional impact of what they had seen along the march, perhaps the order was to be expected.

Soon after they resumed marching, the French units took a left road and the Americans turned right. As the outer British fortifications came into sight across a vast plain, the Baron de Vioménil led the French vanguard under cover of trees. The French established their positions and encampments from the high bank of the river above Yorktown and then curving across the plain to meet the American line. The Americans continued the line eastward all the way back to the shore downstream of the town.

GLOUCESTER 48   WILLIAMSBURG 46   YORKTOWN 47

IN DEFENSE OF THE BRITISH

Yorktown Defenses

As the field officers were seeing to the encampments, Washington used his telescope. He saw formidable but incomplete British fortifications. The town, now hidden by walls, was laid out primarily along one main street and four cross streets, perched on a high bluff above the York River. The settlement of Gloucester lay on a jutting point of land directly across the river. The York

was tidal and two miles wide except where Gloucester Point reduced its width to about a half mile. The only practical way to cross was by boat, and the waters were deep enough for British seaworthy ships to move freely upriver beyond the town.

Closest to the Allied line there were two strong, raised, free-standing redoubts (roofless, defensive earthwork enclosures) on Washington's far right near the downriver bank, and one on his far left, upriver. The latter, known as the Fusiliers Redoubt, was huge and star-shaped, sitting on a high bluff above the banks of the York near the mouth of a creek.

Above the town near the French side of the line and protected by the star-shaped redoubt, British ships anchored close to shore, their cannons trained on the field. Closer to the town than the redoubt, a large creek ravine cut into the land above

Yorktown and then paralleled the town walls about halfway across the plain, forming a superb natural barrier. A bit further from the town on the downriver side was another stream and a great marsh, another partial barrier. The broad central plain was the natural approach, and though it may well have been an attractive shaded meadow once, it was now only a bleak sandy expanse. All along the downriver side of the town, the land ended in a forty-foot sheer drop to the water below. Closer to the town, a series of redoubts and several batteries spread across the plain, and closer still, a line of raised earthwork surrounded the town with seven redoubts and gun batteries strung like beads along it.

Ravines formed a natual barrier to protect the soldiers

Across the river, Washington could see the fort and tents of the British camp at Gloucester. Looking downstream, he could barely see a few of de Grasse's ships just beyond the mouth of the York. Disappointingly, he did not see de Grasse's ships moving upriver because the wind was making sailing in that direction impossible.

Based on what he saw and knew, Washington was confident that the battle could be won, so he ordered 80 siege guns brought to the plain.

Despite the heat, optimism buoyed the Allies as they settled into an armed sleep. The only sounds in the night were the sentries' challenges, axes chopping, and hammers pounding as bridges were built over the marsh.

Behind the British lines, the night was very different. The men were stunned by the vast army before them, and one report estimated that 26,000 enemy were arrayed on the plain. Some responded with fury, eager to fight, but most were terrified. They sniped at the Allies when circumstances allowed, but no attack was sustained. Starting that first night, dozens of deserters made their way toward the American camp.

Early the next day, September 29, the Americans crossed the swamp, shifting camp to the right of the creek to better surround the enemy. The men rapidly dug and built protective trenches to connect each of their guard outposts, while sharpshooters fought off British snipers firing from ravines. The French covered the center and all the way to the upriver side of Yorktown and the Americans covered the right.

Serious fighting began that day. Riflemen killed or injured over 30 Hessian and British soldiers along their outer line of defenses, and in the late afternoon the French repulsed a cavalry unit that then retreated under the cover of cannon fire.

When word came that smallpox was rampant in Yorktown, the sentries were put on high alert to prevent people with the disease from slipping into camp overnight. Focused on barring sick intruders, the Allies were unaware of movement along the British perimeter.

Abandonment of Outer Defenses

Guided by a message received that day, Cornwallis believed they would be rescued within days. Therefore, starting around one in the morning, the British abandoned their entire outer perimeter because the general believed those posts would be unnessary, so defending them would cost lives to no purpose.

By eight in the morning on September 30, the Allies had discovered that all of the major British outer line defenses had been abandoned except for the Fusiliers Redoubt and Redoubts 9 and 10. With no knowledge of the message Cornwallis had received, they were completely mystified, though ecstatic. They now had control of every land access to the town, something they had expected to cost them dearly.

Abandoned British redoubts

Lafayette saw the York River as an escape for Cornwallis

LABORS OF WAR

Preparations for Digging the First Parallel

By afternoon, the Allies were all over the abandoned British line, deepening and flooring trenches, building sites for artillery, fortifying as needed, and raising walls of earth on the Yorktown side. They could see and hear the enemy doing the same inside the British inner defences, some 400 yards and more distant. That same day, French troops tried and failed to take the Fusiliers Redoubt, leaving the upriver approaches still vulnerable to British fire. All through that day and into the next, engineers worked out the layout of the siege lines.

Gabions, one type of moveable fortification

Lafayette worried aloud that Cornwallis might attempt to retreat over the York River. Most of the generals just smiled, dismissive of the very idea, but evidence of conditions dire enough to inspire desperate attempts by the British abounded. On October 1, the Allies learned that the British had slaughtered nearly 700 starving horses. Most of these had been stolen, and their deaths ended some of the best American breeding lines.

Starting on October 1 and continuing unceasingly for a week, most of the army focused on the great task of creating moveable objects needed to make the parallels (man-made siege trenches from which the Allies would fire on Yorktown) and gun emplacements. The whole area became a giant work camp. Over 1,200 men were sent into the woods for thousands of saplings and branches.

These men never knew when they might stumble over another refugee group of starved Blacks, most dead or dying of smallpox. Slender branches were lashed into large bundles called *fascines*, and over 2,000 of them were used to make earthworks. Saplings were woven into 600 huge, open-ended

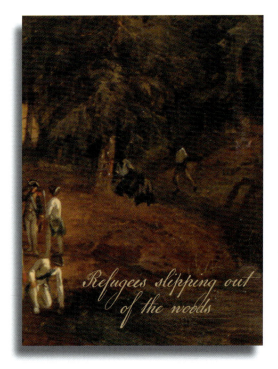

Refugees slipping out of the woods

baskets called *gabions* that would later be filled with dirt to make high walls to protect men in the trenches. They also made 600 *saucisson*s, extra long *fascines*. As they were finished, they were piled along the roads and in the woods, ready for use in the constructing of the parallels.

Simultaneously, the men of other units hauled for miles the siege cannons, mortars, and ammunition that de Barras had brought. It was slow, backbreaking work until heavy draft horses arrived on October 4, after a 400-mile overland drive.

In other places well beyond British range, men sawed and hammered, building artillery platforms that would later go into the parallel trenches yet to be dug. The siege guns would be seated on these, and General Knox had invented a method of tilting the cannons and mortars higher or lower.

At night, whole regiments spread out across the plain to guard the hundreds who were digging the first trenches. They were all exposed and vulnerable, out in the open, so they had good reason to fear for their lives. Yet the British did not attack.

During the day, however, the gunners of Yorktown were active, shooting at every man they saw to prevent the placement of the guns. If the reconnoitering generals tempted them too much, British cavalry would even come tearing out after them. Baiting British artillery became a daredevil sport for some of the troops, but British aim improved and few survived taunting games for long.

On the night of October 2, the slow ten-per-hour British cannon fire suddenly erupted into a furious barrage from the British ships anchored in the river. A short time later, the cannonade abruptly stopped. Though the mystified Allies did not know it, the barrage had been covering the ferrying of Tarleton's Legion to Gloucester, the second front of the siege.

Gloucester Point

On September 28, Lauzun's Legion and hundreds of marines had crossed the York River under the command of General de Choisy to contain the British who were at Gloucester. When they learned Tarleton had come over on the night of the strange barrage, Lauzun and his men could not have been more pleased.

The morning of October 3, word came that Tarleton was in the countryside with a foraging party. The chase was on. The French and Americans soon caught up and engaged the British. Lauzun spotted Tarleton and galloped straight at him, but a wounded horse crashed into Tarleton's mount and both Tarleton and his horse were thrown to the ground. His men rescued him, but as the fight continued, Tarleton and his men retreated, covered by British infantry. Tarleton was wounded, his second-in-command was killed, and a number of soldiers were taken prisoner. From this day on, the second front of the siege was secure; the British units at Gloucester remained contained within their fortifications. No more provisions flowed to Yorktown, and that route of escape was blocked. For the victors, it was a glorious success, and they were celebrated as heroes of the entire Allied Army.

Lauzun Legionnaire

The First Parallel

By the day of Tarleton's defeat, October 3, Cornwallis had 2,000 men incapacitated. He sent another dispatch to Clinton, pleading that river rescue was their only hope.

By October 5, many of the French big guns were in place, and it was time to dig the first trench. That night, cool stormy weather blew in for the first time. Well after dark, a few engineers, sappers (explosive experts), and miners (trench and tunnel makers) ghosted forward through the rain. Directed by the engineers, the men began laying wood strips to mark the edges of the trench to be dug. General Washington silently appeared to approve the placement.

The next day, a gentle, cool rain began to soften the sun-seared earth. Columns of men brought up the *gabions*, *fascines*, and *saucissons*, placing them out in the open no more than 800 yards from the enemy. Meanwhile, several regiments were making even more.

That night Americans lit large campfires near a marshy area and intentionally passed repeatedly and randomly through the light to keep the British focused and firing in the wrong direction. The French also began a false attack on their side at nine o'clock to further distract the enemy from the trenching. To keep the British firing was important because their own noise would keep them from hearing what the Allies were doing.

Weather continued to help the attackers. Twenty-four hours of rain had further softened the ground and continued to blur visibility and muffle sounds. In full dark, the engineers led masses of soldiers carrying trenching tools and materials, and wagons filled with sandbags followed. They stopped where the squad had marked the night before. General Washington hefted one of the pickaxes and struck the earth first before handing over the tool and getting out of the way. All night long they worked to create a four-foot-deep and ten-foot-wide trench that stretched 2,000 yards, from near the center of the plain all the way to the bluff above the downstream shore. Along its length, it was defended by 4 palisaded (walled with upright stakes) redoubts and 5 batteries (gun emplacements). Soldiers also dug a trench leading to a new battery that would allow guns to fire on the British ships above Yorktown.

At dawn on October 7, the British sentries awakened to see the huge fortified line stretched across the plain just beyond musket range, and the British cannons opened up. The Allies suffered casualties but would not be intimidated. They paused work only once to watch as American and French flags were raised. Over the next two days, they continued through the cannon fire, building gun platforms and dragging into place the great guns and finally, ammunition. Never once did the Allies fire a single shot in response.

Fleeing from cannonballs

The Bombardment Begins

The rains stopped on October 9. At three o'clock, the French gunners began placing shots from huge cannons, starting with the British ships that had raked them two days before. Within minutes of the first shot, the British gunship *Guadeloupe* rabbited to the far shore.

Two hours after the French, Washington fired the first American cannon. Cheers rang out up and down the trench, and the chorus of the American guns boomed out. Sergeant Martin, who had been part of the army through all the bleak years, said...

I felt a…pride swell my heart when I saw 'the Star Spangled Banner' waving majestically in the faces of our implacable adversaries; it appeared like an omen of success.

Once the gunners found their range, the howitzers tore apart the enemy placements, and one by one the guns that had been firing against the parallel were destroyed. The Allies' cannonade never stopped that day and through the night, as more and more weapons were brought up and placed. French hotshot (red-hot cannonballs) destroyed several more ships, burning them to the water line.

Johann Doehla, one of the German mercenaries, wrote,

> One could…not avoid the horribly many cannon balls either inside or outside the city. Most… fled with their best possessions…to the bank of the York and dug in among the sand cliffs, but… many were…mortally wounded….

The morning of October 10, an elderly, respected gentleman was released from Yorktown and brought news: Cornwallis was operating out of a cave below the garden, Clinton promised naval rescue, Tarleton was sick, and the British were wretchedly dispirited.

The firing from the parallel never slowed the rest of the day. More than 3,600 shells fell on the town and harbor in the first 24 hours, and the effect was horrific. At least one shot skipped all the way across the broad river and wounded several soldiers on the Gloucester side. People lay everywhere, mortally wounded or dead.

GREATER DANGER, GREATER HONOR

Beginning the Second Parallel and the Taking of Redoubts Nine and Ten

On the clear night of October 11, without any British response, the Allies dug the second parallel, this one 400 yards closer. However, it could not be completed as long as two high, heavily fortified redoubts, Redoubt Number 9 and Redoubt Number 10, were manned by the British. Taking them would be the most dangerous element of the siege.

The French were to take Number 9, located on the Allies' left, a large five-sided structure defended by 120 British soldiers. The Americans were to attack Number 10, slightly smaller and overlooking

the river on the allied right. Seventy enemy soldiers defended it. In total secrecy, each commander picked his unit. Rochambeau gave the high honor to the men of the Royal Deux-Ponts Regiment, led by vicomte Deux-Ponts and assisted by Gatinais pikemen whom de Grasse had transported.

Lafayette had the honor of commanding the Americans and picked Alexander Hamilton to lead the main body. Miners and sappers would first chop a way through the outer barricades while John Laurens's light infantry would cut off rear escape.

At dusk the selected soldiers filed silently into the open field and lay down to wait. Washington spoke simply to them, imploring each to do his best, as the success of the attack depended on these men alone.

The Gatinais men had originally been in the Auvernge Regiment, an ancient, highly respected unit that had been unwillingly swallowed into the Gatinais. The men were pleased at the assignment but were most unhappy at having to risk all without their regimental identity. Rochambeau, who had once been part of the Auvernge, spoke to them, saying,

My children, I have great need of you tonight. I trust you will not forget that we have served together in the brave Regiment of the Auvergne—Auvergne sans tache, the spotless.

He gave his solemn word to work unflinchingly to have the regiment reinstated. The men said that if he would do that, they "will fight like lions…until the last man is killed." As they began to slip out of the trench onto open ground, suddenly many other officers appeared among them, volunteers who would simply not be left behind though already refused by Rochambeau and Washington. They were willing to be punished later for disobeying, but not willing to sit out this battle that fulfilled what they had been trained to do since childhood.

At seven in the evening, the mortar signal was given. A message came down the American line, "Empty your musket." Someone in charge had decided that it was better to send the men in with only bayonets than to risk an accidental firing that would alert the enemy. Not everyone obeyed. The two columns slipped through the darkness. Halfway to its assigned redoubt, the American column stopped and a "Forlorn Hope" unit was formed with one man from each company. These twenty would lead over the wall. John Laurens's unit left the column to circle around behind the redoubt. Sappers raced forward and began shattering the silence with mighty axe blows against the tangled wooden mantraps around the redoubt.

A British soldier shouted a challenge. No voice answered, and the British soldier fired. Huzzahs rang from the Americans, and the British line opened fire. The Forlorn Hope unit forced through the tangled branches, across the dry moat, past the sharpened stakes, over the palisade and in. Some made it. Captain Stephen Olney, a Rhode Island veteran who had been in service since the beginning of the war, made it in and called his men to form up. As he did, several British soldiers slashed him with bayonets. As one soldier was about to deliver the killing blow, one of Olney's men shot the enemy with the musket ball he had refused to remove from his weapon. The battle ended quickly, and most of the enemy soldiers surrendered. With a loss of 9 dead and 25 wounded, the Americans had taken Redoubt Number 10.

The French were challenged before even reaching the outer defense. "*Wer da?* (*Who's there?*)" a Hessian sentry called out. Bullets poured down upon the French soldiers as they raced forward, only to find that they could not get through the enmeshed tree limbs surrounding the redoubt base. As sappers chopped, the French soldiers coolly returned fire. A Deux-Ponts man, Georg Daniel Flohr, described the scene, "they fired so heavily at us from out of the redoubt that we fell just like snowflakes." Once the French were in, however, they were so fierce that the place was theirs in seven minutes. It was the Gatinais, the ancient Auvergne, under the leadership of the marquis de Rostaing, who led and fought like lions at the cost of a full third of their number. Upon his return to France, "Papa" Rochambeau kept his word to his men, and the Auvergne Regiment was reinstated. Redoubt Number 9 was bought with the price of 15 French lives and 57 wounded.

Inside Yorktown, the sound of the battles and the roars of the men raised the level of fear to a new pitch. One soldier estimated an attack force of at least 3,000 men that sounded like the Wild Hunt, a terrifying event from European mythology.

LAST ACTS · VICTORY

Countermeasures

The British forces launched a powerful counteroffensive barrage, killing or injuring over 500 men. Nonetheless, when the sun rose on October 15, the Allies' howitzers were in the redoubts facing the enemy, and the parallel extended all the way to the downstream shore. Its nearest point was within 150 yards of the British inner line, point blank range.

Cornwallis kept up the pounding, but he saw the inevitable. The coded letter he sent out on that day said,

> The safety of the place is, therefore, so precarious that I cannot recommend that the fleet and army should run great risk in endeavouring to save us.

He was ready for desperate measures.

Starting in the middle of that night, the British began heavy bombardment, and the firing did not abate. Around four in the morning, a unit attacked the new parallel. They killed and injured sleeping soldiers and spiked cannon after cannon until vicomte de Noailles led a violent charge that pushed them back to their lines. The British action had been brave, but futile. By midmorning on October 16, all the damaged guns and more were blazing. The survivors in Yorktown simply could not believe it.

Cornwallis finally decided to attempt what Lafayette had predicted. During the day, he sent all the injured and sick across to Gloucester. Late that night, during massive covering fire from British ships, their army began to cross the river. Cornwallis planned to go with the second wave. Most of the first thousand had made the crossing, and boats were reloading when a violent storm blew in and thrashed the river into a destructive maelstrom for hours, swamping and scattering the escape vessels downstream.

Final Moves

Under the cover of the storm, the Americans and French built and armed another section of trench, this one so close that a soldier could almost have lobbed a rock into the British line. The morning of October 17, the Allies' guns began firing against both land and ships, and Cornwallis abandoned the retreat. Not a single British cannon fired back. The outer walls of Yorktown were ready to fall; only about 3,000 soldiers were still functioning, and the French fleet was ready to sail into firing range. There was no way for the British to win, no place to go, no hope of rescue. "Under all these circumstances I thought it would have been wanton and inhuman to…sacrifice the lives of this small body of gallant soldiers," Cornwallis later wrote.

Around nine that morning, a red-coated boy stepped onto a parapet and began a drum roll that could not be heard until he was noticed and the guns went silent. An officer stepped onto the plain carrying a white handkerchief. The boy climbed down and walked forward with him, beating the "parlay" signal. The officer was blindfolded and led through the Allies' lines and into a house well back, while the soldiers watched silently. In that house, Washington read the letter the man had brought from Cornwallis.

> *Sir I propose cessation of hostilities for twenty-four hours, and that two officers may be appointed by each side, to meet at Mr. Moore's house, to settle terms for the surrender of the posts at York and Gloucester.*

Both sides waited to see what would happen.

At noon, the man was led back past the lines and allowed to take off the blindfold. The minute he was within Yorktown walls, the Allies' cannons resumed, but three hours later, again they stopped for another messenger, this one with Washington's reply. Washington gave Cornwallis two hours to submit his requested terms in writing. The British commander complied, requesting that his men be sent back to their native land with all their private property.

Washington dismissed that request out of hand, but agreed to more hours without barrage to work out terms. He also sent a message to de Grasse, asking him to come. While four high-ranking officers, two for the British and Laurens and Noailles for the Allies, negotiated on behalf of their commanders, the British used that night to destroy ships, ammunition, and most every other thing of value. The Allies simply waited.

A serenade of bagpipes from Yorktown ushered in the morning of October 18, and the French musicians replied in kind. As the sun rose, thousands of French and American soldiers stood atop their works. Across the torn ground, they could see the English officers assembled on the parapets of Yorktown, and below on the riverbank the hundreds of civilians huddled. Wrecked ships listed in the water, and far beyond them to the east they could see two great French ships gliding up the river under full sail, edged in sunlight. By noon, the French ships were anchored near the wrecks.

Terms of Surrender

On the morning of October 19, 1781, in Redoubt Number 10, Washington, Rochambeau, and de Barras (asthma forced de Grasse to remain aboard his ship) received and signed the Articles of Capitulation already signed by Cornwallis.

Necessary Roughness

The surrender terms were generous. The surrender ceremony, however, was harsh and intentionally humiliating to the British. It had to be because of the way this same army had treated the Continentals at every opportunity. Washington knew full well that Britain, and indeed

every other European nation,
As the commander-in-chief, he had
by returning honor for honor and
did not like it, but the message was

That same morning, October 19,
British fleet finally sailed from New

By early afternoon, the Allies
surrender. From Williamsburg and
well. The ceremony was solemn,
importance of the event, and the

considered itself superior to America.
to demand and enforce their respect
dishonor for dishonor. The British
understood.

after a month spent on repairs, the
York harbor to rescue Cornwallis.

were assembled on the field of
miles around, civilians gathered as
awe-inspiring, and befitting the
onlookers were kept well back.

Ceremony

Along one side of the road from Yorktown, the American army stood shoulder-to-shoulder two lines deep. In front were the Continentals, and behind them stood the militia. Facing

them were the French regiments, creating a corridor between the two armies close to a mile long. At the head of the two columns, nearest Yorktown, the commanders were on horseback: Washington, Lincoln, Lafayette, and the other generals on the American side, and Rochambeau, Vioménil, de Barras, and the rest of the French Command across from them.

At the far end of the line, Lauzun's Legion closed the corridor with a great semi-circle within which the surrendering soldiers would lay down their weapons and gear. Officers were allowed to keep their sabers, but they and common soldiers and sailors gave up all else except any knapsacks. From this surrender field, the vanquished returned, physically and mentally reduced, to the Yorktown garrison.

Among the Allies, all soldiers, sailors, and marines were dressed as neatly as they could manage, the French resplendent and the Americans ranging from well-dressed officers to barefoot men in rags. None could miss the contrast, but the French soldiers knew by then the measure of the Americans and regarded them with respect. Baron von Closen's thoughts were:

> ...most of these unfortunate persons were clad in small jackets of white cloth, dirty and ragged, and a number of them were almost barefoot.... What does it matter!... These people are much more praise-worthy to fight as they do, when they are so poorly supplied with everything.

The French musicians played lively music as they waited, and the American colors and French standards waved high.

Finally there was a roll of drums from Yorktown. The armed British columns emerged, marching with furled flags at a slow pace as their band played melancholy British tunes rather than the American military music that tradition dictated.

General Cornwallis was absent. General Charles O'Hara, second-in-command, led. Comte de Dumas rode out to guide the defeated column through the silent lines of soldiers.

The British and Hessians were sharply dressed in new uniforms, but it was clear that some were drunk. Officers among them led with tearing eyes.

As they reached the commanders, O'Hara offered his sword to Rochambeau, who shook his head and pointed across to Washington, saying, "We are all subordinate to the Americans. General Washington will give you orders."

O'Hara bowed and turned to Washington with an apology for his "mistake." He stated his identity and that he represented Cornwallis, who was indisposed. Again he started to offer his sword, but Washington politely told him to offer it to General Lincoln, his second–in–command. Lincoln accepted the sword, held it for a few seconds, and ceremoniously returned it. Then he directed O'Hara to the great circle of hussars who told him how his army should proceed.

As the soldiers marched, Lafayette noted that the British refused to look at the Americans. He understood and would not tolerate this insult. He got word to the musicians. At the proper moment, as they suddenly burst into "Yankee Doodle" (a well-known tune that the Patriots had changed from a British insult to a Patriot celebration), the startled British eyes snapped up, straight at the men who for six long years had suffered to make this day a reality.

Except for the music, the whole march was almost silent. At the moment of relinquishing their arms and gear, however, mortification, rage, and sorrow overcame many career soldiers. Losing to American citizen soldiers—farmers and shopkeepers—devastated them.

Across the river, the same ceremony took place in miniature in Gloucester. The only comfort for British, Hessians, and Loyalists came from their realization that it was this or death.

YORKTOWN 47   GLOUCESTER 48   NEW YORK CITY 26

AFTERMATH

The Gentlemanly Art of War

According to European military protocol, leaders of both sides were expected to host their opponents at formal dinners following a surrender. The Americans found the very idea repulsive, but because their French allies believed it to be important, Washington reluctantly agreed. On the very night of the surrender, Washington had to host the first dinner. This tradition caused more estrangement between the Allies than anything in all the preceding months. The fact that the French officers so obviously enjoyed the company of the British appalled the Americans, and some said so. The awkward reality was that the European officers had more in common with each other than they did with American generals. For most of them, leading troops in war was a gentlemanly endeavor, a noble sport that allowed one to attain glory and status important "in society." Nothing about this war had ever been sport to Americans. Captain Ewald of the Hessians noted:

> *General Washington...cast stern expressions toward the French generals over the too-friendly relations between the French and our officers. He ordered the French guards relieved by Americans at both posts. We still enjoyed much courtesy from our opponent's side, but a cool conduct began to prevail among the two divers nations which, in good fortune, had formed only one.*

News of Victory

Washington wrote Congress as soon as he could leave the dinner. His report understated his part and heaped praise upon others. Very early the next morning, October 20, thirty-seven-year-old Tench Tilghman, an officer whom Washington deeply admired, pretended to be well so he could accept the honor of delivering the message.

Rochambeau sent his report to the French Minister of War, and gave the honor of taking it to the duc de Lauzun, who sailed on October 24. As insurance, Rochambeau sent the same message with the comte de Deux-Ponts on another ship two days later. Both ships arrived in record time.

In a congratulatory letter to Rochambeau emblazoned with his seal and personal signature, the King wrote the very day he learned of the victory:

In calling these events to mind and in acknowledging how much the abilities of General Washington, your talents, those of the general officers under both of you, and the valor of the troops, have rendered this campaign glorious, my chief purpose is to inspire in the hearts of all as well as in my own the deepest gratitude toward the Author of all prosperity....And I beseech God to keep you under His holy protection.

Tilghman, dangerously ill, showed up at the Philadelphia home of Thomas McKean, President of Congress, well after midnight on October 23. He pounded on the door so loudly that the night watchman rushed over to arrest the unsteady man he assumed to be drunk when at last McKean opened the door. Tilghman made his delivery before collapsing. The watchman continued his rounds crying out, "Past dree o'glock und Cornvallis ist tagen!" Soon bells rang out across the city, and continued through the rest of the night.

Tighlman was received as a hero. A day of national thanksgiving was proclaimed. Soon thereafter, he and an aide who had arrived with the captured regimental colors (flags) headed a grand parade to lay the flags at the feet of Congress. It was solemn and wonderful, and followed by special church services. The same level of excitement and thankful celebration was echoed throughout the nation.

In France, the celebrations were even grander and deeply heartfelt by everyone. In the palace, avenging national honor and strategic gains were the main causes for joy. The people of France were celebrating also because they had come to love the very idea of America.

Cornwallis Dealing with Defeat

On the day after the surrender, October 20, Cornwallis wrote to London of his humiliating loss, blaming Clinton entirely. Next he filled every usable inch of the one "unsearched" ship he had been granted with 250 Loyalists and defectors. On October 22, it set sail for New York. That done, he was "well" and ready to face his enemies with grace, as dictated by military protocol.

IMMEDIATE IMPACT

Too Little, Too Late

The same day that Philadelphia learned of the victory, October 23, 1781, the British navy arrived off the Chesapeake Bay. Graves learned of the surrender from men who rowed out to his ship, and the admiral promptly sailed the fleet straight back to New York. When the ships disappeared from view, the Allies knew the battle was truly at an end.

Wrap-Up and Preparation

As gratifying as this victory was, the war continued in the rest of the country. The British held not only New York City but also Wilmington, Charleston, Savannah, and Saint Augustine. Thirty thousand British soldiers were spread between Florida and Maine, and more were beyond the mountains. The French fleet had been essential but would be leaving within days. Surely the British navy would return, perhaps more powerful than ever before. There was much to do before they did.

First, the Americans needed to take the captured soldiers and the trove of military equipment out of reach. Militiamen marched the prisoners off to the military prisons in West Virginia and Maryland the second morning after the surrender.

Washington also had to get his army back to the North. Admiral de Grasse agreed to stay long enough to transport military equipment, supplies, and Washington's men back to Head of Elk, an incalculable service. By November 3, the laden ships were underway.

The commanders hoped that the French fleet would return to the Chesapeake in May 1782, gather up the French army, and with the Continentals, retake New York in June. The French army would winter around Williamsburg.

Personal Tragedy

Washington did not leave with his army on the transports. The night of the surrender he had learned that his stepson Jackie Custis was gravely ill 50 miles up the York River. As soon as he completed tasks that only he could handle, he rode swiftly and arrived just hours before his son died. Washington stayed the week, comforting Martha and being comforted.

Jackie Custis

The American Army of the North, Late 1781–1782

Washington's army traveled back to the Hudson Highlands by approximately the same routes they had taken south. They were buoyed by success and treated extraordinarily well every step of the way. Back at their camps, they were well led and provisioned through the winter, but Washington himself had to work with Congress in Philadelphia until late March 1782, when, with Martha, he rejoined his army.

Rochambeau's Army in Williamsburg

In Virginia, the French soldiers were so disciplined, respectful, charming, and well funded that they overcame local reservations. Rochambeau was anxious to return to France, but led with consummate professionalism as the months dragged. During this period, he received both official and personal letters of thanks and praise from the states and from individual Americans. All thanked him, France, and his soldiers for their invaluable help and sacrifices, but the State of Maryland thanked him in addition for dispelling the generations of misunderstanding and prejudice against the French. (Minister de Luzerne also gave him full credit for this remarkable accomplishment.) He kept these letters, though he could not understand the words. Years later, during the dark days of the French Revolution, he painstakingly translated them.

Immediate Impact in New York City

In New York City, news of Cornwallis's surrender was a profound blow to all but the Patriots. Loyalists besieged headquarters for protection and some made plans to emigrate. Camaraderie within the British command was destroyed by anger, blame casting, and defensiveness.

Immediate Impact in London

When Lord North, the powerful minister who had prosecuted this war, learned of the surrender, he reacted violently. According to Lord Germain, the man who delivered the message, "He reeled, threw out his arms, exclaiming wildly, as he paced up and down... 'Oh God! It's all over!'"

King George III may have been the last to understand the importance of the loss. Anti-war sentiment was so strong in England and the nation brought so low by the loss that Lord North's power base disappeared almost overnight. The Yorktown news arrived in November right before a legislative recess. When Parliament reconvened in February, the House of Commons voted against further prosecution of the "offensive war" in the Colonies, and a few days later the legislators authorized the King to make peace.

With deepest appreciation

Rochambeau and the French Army Depart

Until a British cessation of hostilities was offered and accepted, the war continued. In the spring of 1782, the Allies decided to relocate French forces northward toward Boston. In late June 1782, parts of Rochambeau's army began the trek, but the heat was already so dangerous that most of the army remained near Baltimore until late August.

As the French army basically retraced their southward route, Rochambeau and his senior staff rode to Philadelphia to meet with General Washington and attend the French Ambassador's ball. Though the gala officially celebrated the birth of the prince of France, it was also a victory celebration. While there, the generals decided both armies should take positions in or near the Hudson Highlands. Orders were sent to all locations of French troops. As swiftly as possible, all were on the way to New York, and their journeys were often lightened by celebrations given by towns along the route.

In October, almost a year after the Yorktown victory, Washington and the Continentals honored the French army at King's Ferry, New York, playing French marches as Rochambeau and his men passed between columns of Americans. This night was a farewell, and Washington expressed his gratitude, affection, and admiration with deep feeling. Shipping so many men and so much equipment took time, but Rochambeau and the last of the French Expeditionary Force departed from the United States in early 1783.

Though Americans were greatly relieved that the foreign soldiers left, with few exceptions, the French had earned goodwill and respect everywhere they went. Washington's relationship with Lafayette continued to strengthen and was graced with return visits. Rochambeau and Washington maintained their friendship through correspondence all their lives.

Washington felt deeply the bond and the debt of honor he and America owed. Whenever appropriate, he made sure others remembered as well. On the anniversary of the inception of the Alliance that February, the password and countersign he assigned for that day were...

America and France

to be answered by

United Forever

Lasting Impact

The men of France enriched and expanded the thoughts of Americans, and America in turn influenced the French. Seeing the daily use of Enlightenment ideals of self-governance, the rule of law that protected natural and inalienable rights, mutual respect, hard work, civic responsibility, honor, virtue, and opportunity for self-improvement was deeply impressive to men who had always lived under the rule of kings and nobles. As the time for departure drew near, the lure of America was so strong that precautions had to be taken against desertions by common soldiers whose future in France offered less promise. Many officers, though not tempted to stay, went home committed to achieving for France American liberties. Colonel de Ségur later wrote in his memoirs, "We were all dreaming of Liberty...and we were destined to bring home the germs of an ardent passion for emancipation and independence." The results in France started with high ideals. Unfortunately, the people lacked experience with self-government and fanatics gained control for a period. In a letter to Washington written from his country home, April, 1790, during the French Revolution, Rochambeau explained the reason for the difference between the American Revolution and the tragic events unfolding in France by writing:

> Do you remember, my dear General, of the first repast we made together at Rod Island? I made you remark from the Soup the difference of character of our two Nations, the French burning their throats and all the Americans waiting wisely the time it was cooled! I believe, my dear General, you have seen since a year that our Nation has not changed character. We go very fast. God will that we reach our aim.

In time, France did find its way to a stable constitutional government. For several decades, though, European interests and conflicts strained the relationship between France and the young United States. Through those years, however, personal bonds between Americans and Frenchmen survived, and eventually ties between the nations of France and America once again grew strong.

The Siege of Yorktown

Outstanding men ~ Washington, Rochambeau, Lafayette, de Grasse, Hamilton, Duportail, Laurens, and countless others ~ came together on the plain of Yorktown. The Alliance created a bond that would hold strong through the centuries.

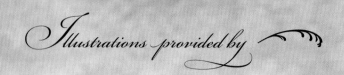

Illustrations provided by

A special thank you to Barbara R. Trathen, Editor; Lauren Smulcer, Editor; Lt. Col. (ret.) Ron Olney, PhD, military historian, Editor; and to Brian Willson of OldFonts.com

The selective, annotated bibliography can be found with the documents portal at www.valuesthroughhistory.org

Historic Sites to Visit along the Washington Rochambeau Revolutionary Route (W3R)

(After the name of each town, see the corresponding number from the foldout map)

Along the historic trail, many historic sites, tours, and interactive experiences can be found. The list below includes some of the authors' favorites. For more comprehensive lists of sites with maps, directions, historic markers, please refer to the following websites.

National Park Service—https://www.nps.gov/waro/planyourvisit/directions.htm

W3R—https://www.w3r-us.org

Dr. Robert A. Selig has written detailed articles covering all aspects of the Alliance and routes, many of which are available online through the websites listed above.

Many of the sites listed below also have their own websites that include schedules and special events, and we suggest your checking those as part of your planning. Additionally, by researching guided tours in locales you intend to visit, you may find just the tour for you. We have also included a very few charming inns in states along the trail that have continuously been functioning since the Revolution or before. These are delightful places to stay and dine today just as travelers in the 18th century America favored them.

Connecticut

ANDOVER (BOLTON) Map Point 6

Daniel White's Tavern, 131 Hutchinson Rd.—Opened as a tavern in 1773 by Daniel White, a Coventry selectman and an army captain during the Revolutionary War. Known as White's Tavern at the Sign of the Black Horse, a frequent stopping place for the comte de Rochambeau during the war.

ESSEX – INN No Map Point

The Griswold Inn, 36 Main Street. 860.767.1776—One of the oldest continuously operated inns in the country, it opened its doors in the picturesque and historic seaport village of Essex in 1776, near the banks of the Connecticut River. Excellent food and lodging as well as museum quality artwork, and a collection of firearms primarily from the American Revolution and/or the War of 1812.

FARMINGTON Map Point 10

Farmington Historical Society, 138 Main St. 860.674.9931—Research, exhibits, and reinactment events

LEBANON Map Point 16

Jonathan Trumbull House and surrounding buildings, 169 W. Town St.—home of the only Colonial Governor to support the war for independence, and the birthplace of John Trumbull, America's Patriot artist. CT-DAR property

Trumbull War Office, 149 W. Town Street—SAR property

Lebanon Historical Society Museum and Visitors Center, on Historic Lebanon Green, 856 Trumbull Hwy.

MIDDLEBURY (BREAKNECK/WATERBURY) Map Point 12

Josiah Bronson Tavern, 506 Breakneck Hill Rd.—Served as a tavern and billet for French officers June 27-July 1, 1781 and again October 26-28, 1782. One of the officers was General Rochambeau's second in command during the Yorktown campaign, Baron de Vioménil. Rochambeau himself most likely stayed with Captain Isaac Bronson, Josiah's father, further down the hill.

WETHERSFIELD (Wethersford) Map Point 9

Webb-Deane-Stevens Museum, 211 Main St. 860.529.0612—Three meticulously restored homes including the 1752 Joseph Webb House that served as Washington's headquarters in May 1781. Visitors today will see the home handsomely restored to its later Federal period appearance.

Delaware

NEWWARK No Map Point

Cooch's Bridge Monument, Old Baltimore Pike, east of Rt. 896, between 896 & Rt. 72, Newark—Explanatory plaques of the only battle that took place in Delaware.

Maryland

ANNAPOLIS No Map Point

Colonial Annapolis Historic District, Bounded by Spa Creek, Southgate Ave., Hanover & West Sts. 800.978.3370—Indoor and outdoor tours of historically significant 18th century buildings and homes, as well as St. Anne's Church and Maryland State House, where Washington resigned his military position, but buy tickets early.

United States Naval Academy, 121 Blake Rd.—Outstanding, admission rules apply; museum, crypt of John Paul Jones.

BALTIMORE Map Point 42

Mount Clare Mansion, 1500 Washington Blvd. 410.837.3262—House museum, built as home of Charles Carroll and Margaret Tighlman Carroll, leading patriots; NSCDA property; multiple programs.

CROWNSVILLE No Map Point

Scott's House/Belvoir (six miles from Annapolis)—Great estate and magnificent 18th century home. Rochambeau's army encamped on the estate, and Lafayette stayed in the main house during his return trip in 1824. Contact the Historic Annapolis Foundation for information about access.

ELKTON (Head of Elk) Map Point 41

Partridge Hill, Main St.—Home of Henry Hollingsworth, commissary for the Eastern Shore who obtained supplies for the Allies who embarked from there in 1781.

PERRYVILLE (Lower Ferry) No Map Point

Principio Iron Works, 1723 Principio Furnace Rd. 410.642.9213—Maker of cannon balls for the Continental Army. Call ahead for tour.

Rodgers Tavern, 259 Broad St. 410.642.6066—Tavern owned by Patriot John Rodgers next to Lower Ferry, an important Susquehanna River crossing used en route to Virginia in 1781; Washington et al stayed there en route to New York regularly.

Massachusetts

BOSTON Map Point 1

Boston National Historic Park—Myriad key Revolutionary tours and sites

Freedom Trail—Fascinating walking trail with audio guide that starts at Boston Common

LEXINGTON–CONCORD No Map Point

NPS Minute Man National Historic Park, Rt. 2A-West, 1 mile west of Massachusetts Turnpike—Outstanding experience

SUDBURY – INN No Map Point

Longfellow's Wayside Inn—Men in Sudbury came to the aid of Concord on April 19, 1775, and 90 years later Longfellow recited the famous poem, "Paul Revere's Ride" at the inn. Wednesday evenings the Sudbury Ancient Fife and Drum Corp comes marching through the inn. Excellent food and lodging; perfect for visiting Lexingon/Concord as well as Boston.

New Jersey

HACKENSACK (River Edge) No Map Point

Historic New Bridge Landing—Walking tour area to which Washington's army fled across the Hackensack River in November of 1776. Historic buildings, including the Zabriskie-Steuben House, 1209 Main St. 201.343.9492

MORRISTOWN Map Point 32

Morristown National Historic Park and Washington Headquarters Museum, 30 Washington Pl. 973.543.4030—Tours and events at three sites: Jockey Hollow Visitors Center, Ford Mansion, Fort Nonsense

The Green, bounded by West, North, East, & South Pl.—Historic signs and statues

PRINCETON Map Point 35

Princeton Battlefield State Park, 500 Mercer Rd. 609.921.0074—Highlights: Battlefield site, Clarke House Museum.

RIDGEWOOD No Map Point

Old Paramus Reformed Church, 39 acres 201.444.5933—Site of a Continental Army military post for four years. In the original church building, Washington held the court-martial of General Charles Lee in 1778. Washington headquartered at the church ten times in 1778-1780. Alexander Hamilton, Lafayette, Anthony Wayne, Richard Henry Lee, and Aaron Burr also were here.

SPRINGFIELD Map Point 30

Presbyterian Church, 210 Morris Ave.—Church from which the Patriots were supplied with Watts hymnals to use for wadding by Rev. Caldwell who made famous his words, "Give them Watts, boys!" during the Battle of Springfield in June, 1780.

New York

BEDFORD Map Point 14

John Jay Homestead, 400 Jay St., Katonah 914.232.5651—Camps and events

CROTON-ON-HUDSON No Map Point

Van Courtlandt Manor, 525 S. Riverside Ave. 914.366.6900—Living history of domestic life of a patriot family

FORT MONTGOMERY No Map Point

Fort Montgomery State Historic Site, 690 Route 9West 845.446.2134—Patriot fort overrun on October 6, 1777 by British, Loyalist and Hessian forces trying to force their way up to Saratoga. Living history events

NEWBURGH No Map Point

Washington's Headquarters, 84 Liberty St. 845.562.1195—Here Washington rejected the idea that he should be king after the war, preventing military control of the government; created and awarded the Badge of Military Merit, forerunner to the Purple Heart. Museum, guided tours, historical programs

NEW WINDSOR Map Point 23

New Windsor Cantonment Historic Site, 374 Temple Hill Rd. 845.561.1765—Winter and spring encampment of Washington's units of the Continental Army during the last year of war. Here Washington issued the ceasefire orders on April 19, 1783; contains the National Purple Heart Hall of Honor, the Temple of Virtue, General Knox's New Windsor Artillery Park, and an original hut; live programs

STONY POINT No Map Point

Stony Point Battlefield State Historic Site, 44 Battlefield Rd. 845.786-2521—Continental Army reinactments and more

WEST POINT Map Point 22

United States Military Academy, 845.446.4724 or westpointtours.com—Critically important fortress that Arnold betrayed; rules of admission apply.

YORKTOWN (Crompond) No Map Point

The town of Crompond renamed itself Yorktown and hosted the French 1782.

Pennsylvania

CHADDS FORD No Map Point

Brandywine Battlefield Park, 1 mile east of Chadds Ford on US 1—Battle of Brandywine tours; museum in Washington's headquarters.

PHILADELPHIA Map Point 37

Carpenters Hall, 320 Chestnut St. 215.925.0167—Site of Franklin and Jay's secret meetings with French agent Bonvouloir in 1775.

City Tavern, 138 S 2nd St. 215.413.1443—Restaurant serving period foods in replica of the "most genteel tavern in America" in which many American Revolution events took place, including Washington's first meeting with Lafayette.

Constitution Center, 525 Arch St. 215.409.6600—Outstanding multimedia programs, exhibits and hands-on experiences

Franklin Court, Chestnut and Market Streets between 3rd and 4th Sts. 215.965.2305—Museum, printing office

Independence Hall, 520 Chestnut St.—Declaration of Independence and United States Constitution debated and adopted here; displays, tours, events

Independence Visitors Center, 41 N. 6th St.—Film presentations, tickets

Liberty Bell Center, 526 Market Street—Liberty Bell, film and exhibits

Museum of the American Revolution, 123 Chestnut St. 215.253.6731—Powerful interactive American Revolution experience; Washington's headquarters tent and famous seige of Yorktown painting are among many treasures.

New Hall Military Museum, in Carpenters Court next to Carpenters Hall—Exhibits, tours regarding Continental Marines, Army, and Navy in building of War Department

Second Bank, 420 Chestnut St.—Portrait gallery of heroes of the American Revolution, many by Charles Willson Peale

Valley Forge National Historical Park, 1400 Outer Line Dr., King of Prussia 610.783.1099—Film, museum, tours, interactive reinactments, and much more

WASHINGTON CROSSING No Map Point

Washington Crossing Historic Park, 1112 River Rd. 215.493.4076—Visitor center, guided tours, historic buildings, boat, etc

Rhode Island

COVENTRY No Map Point

Nathan Hale Homestead, 2299 South St.

Waterman's Tavern, 283 Maple Valley Rd.—French encampment site June 18-22, 1781 & November, 1782 encampment; guided

NEWPORT Map Point 2

Brick Market Museum of Newport History and Shop, 127 Thames St. 401.841.8770—Active market through the French encampment; guided walking tours

French Campsites July, 1780–November 1780—Main army camped along the coast bounded by Spring Street and Thames Street; Lauzun's men were at Castle Hill.

Friends Meeting House, 30 Marlborough St.—Used as the French hospital

Homes: Homes of the period—at least twenty-five were quarters of French officers, including: ***Hunter House***, 54 Washington St.—quarters and place of death of Admiral de Ternay; ***William Vernon House***, 46 Clark St.—Rochambeau's headquarters

Rochambeau Plaza, Wellington Ave.—Landing site with many markers

Touro Synagogue, 72 Touro St.—Oldest United States synagogue, dating from 1763

Town Prison, 13 Marlborough St.

Trinity Church Cemetery, 44 Church St.—Tomb marker of Admiral de Ternay

PROVIDENCE Map Point 3 Cranston St. & Broad St.—In use June 12-22, 1781 & November 9-16, 1782

Governor Stephen Hopkins House, Hopkins St. at Benefit St.

University Hall, Brown University—French hospital June 25, 1780–May 27, 1782

Virginia

ALEXANDRIA No Map Point

Christ Church, 118 N Washington St. 703.549.1450—Guided tours

Gadsby's Tavern, 134 N Royal St. 703.746.4242—18th c. restaurant, period cuisine & entertainment; attached museum

Ferry Farm, 268 Kings Hwy. 540.370.0732—Childhood home of George Washington

CHARLOTTESVILLE No Map Point

Monticello, 931 Thomas Jefferson Parkway 434.984.9800—Thomas Jefferson's estate, offering outstanding exhibits, tours, and events all designed to bring to life the extraordinary time, life, accomplishments, and character of this complex and gifted man

FREDERICKSBURG No Map Point

Hugh Mercer Apothecary, 1020 Caroline St. 540.373.3362—Museum of pharmacy, medicine, and 18th century politics; costumed interpreters

Kenmore, 1201 Washington Ave. 540.373.3381—Home of Washington's sister and her husband, a merchant and Patriot.

Mary Washington House, 1200 Charles St. 540.373.1569—Home of George Washington's mother; tours, costumed interpreters

Rising Sun Tavern, 1304 Caroline St. 540.371.1494—Home of Charles Washington, younger brother of George Washington, became a tavern in 1792. Lively tour

GLOUCESTER POINT Map Point 48

Tendall's Point Park, 1376 Vernon St.—Site of Gloucester surrender

LORTON No Map Point

Gunston Hall, 10709 Gunston Rd. 703-550.9220—An elegant Georgian home museum of leading Patriot scholar, legislator, and author of the Virginia Declaration of Rights, George Mason. Tours, costumed interpreters, programs

MOUNT VERNON Map Point 43

George Washington's Mount Vernon, 3200 Mount Vernon Hwy. 703.780.2000—An extaordinary engaging experience at one of the nation's most beloved historic sites, honoring George Washington's life and legacy, worth at least a full day's visit

WILLIAMSBURG Map Point 46

College of William and Mary, 102 Richmond Rd. 757.221.4000—Tours, events

Colonial Williamsburg, 888.965.7254—Extraordinary living history experience that can last for days

YORKTOWN Map Point 47

Yorktown Battlefield Visitors Center, 1000 Colonial Pkwy. 757.898.2410—the only way to fully grasp the events of the siege of Yorktown.

Watermen's Museum, 309 Water St. 757.887.2641—Features crucial roles of watermen during the American Revolution

American Revolution Museum at Yorktown, 200 Water St. 888.593.4682—Much to see and do, including an experiential theater that transports visitors to the Siege of Yorktown with wind, smoke and the thunder of cannon fire.

ATLANTIC OCEAN

LONG ISLAND

BUZZARDS BAY

Boston Harbor

1. Encampments... 🟫 🟦
2. Town... ⛪
3. Route of most of Allied columns.... ────
4. Route of Lauzun's screening force... ────

...beau *Revolutionary Route*

General Rochambeau's Campaign Map

Locations:

New Windsor 25
West Point 22
Newburgh
Verplank
Kings Ferry
Haverstraw 24
Pompton 31
Whippany
Peekskill
Cromond
Hunt's Tavern
Pines Bridge
Salem
Paramus 28
North Castle (Mount Kisko) 15
Danbury
Salem
New Town 13
Breakneck (Middlebury) 12
Waterbury
Southington 11
Farmington 10
PHILADELPHIA 37
Red Lions (Frankford)
Bristol
Bullions Tavern (Liberty Corner) 33
Morristown (Millstone) 32
Chatham 29
Somerset Courthouse 34
Springfield 30
Scot's Plan (Scotch Plains) 27
Trenton 36
Princeton 35
Dobbs Ferry 25
Hackensack
NEW YORK 26
Philipsburg 21
Bedford 14
Ridgebury
Ridgefield 10
North Stratford (Trumbull)
New Town
Hartford 8
East Hartford 7
Wethersford 9
Oxford (Derby) 19
Wallingsford 18
Middle Town 17
New Stratford (Monroe)
New Haven
Haddam
Andover/Bolton 6
Windham 5
Lebanon 16
Staten Island
Plainsfield/Wollantown 4
Waterman's Tavern (Coventry)
Wrentham
Dedham
Lexington 1
BOSTON
PROVIDENCE 2
NEWPORT 2
Boston Harbor 3

This 18th century map of routes for a marching army
does not include state borders or adhere to
exact north-south orientation.